A Brief Colorado Indian History of the 1800s

Through a Factual Lens

Other books by Roberta Carol Harvey from Sunstone Press:

The Earth Is Red: The Imperialism of the Doctrine of Discovery

The Eclipse of the Sun: The Need for American Indian Curriculum in High Schools

The Iron Triangle: Business, Government, and Colonial Settlers' Dispossession of Indian Timberlands and Timber

All That Glitters Is Ours: The Theft of Indian Mineral Resources

Social Contributions of Colorado's American Indian Leaders

Warrior Societies A Manifesto

The Empty Breadbasket: The Theft of Indian Agricultural Lands

A BRIEF COLORADO INDIAN HISTORY OF THE 1800S

Through a Factual Lens

Roberta Carol Harvey

A Citizen of the Navajo Nation

Sunstone Press
Santa Fe

© 2024 by Roberta Carol Harvey
All Rights Reserved
No part of this book may be reproduced in any form or by any electronic or mechanical means including information storage and retrieval systems without permission in writing from the publisher, except by a reviewer who may quote brief passages in a review.

Sunstone books may be purchased for educational, business, or sales promotional use.
For information please write: Special Markets Department, Sunstone Press,
P.O. Box 2321, Santa Fe, New Mexico 87504-2321.
Printed on acid-free paper
∞

Library of Congress Cataloging-in-Publication Data

Names: Harvey, Roberta Carol, 1950- author.
Title: A brief Colorado Indian history of the 1800s : through a factual lens / Roberta Carol Harvey, a citizen of the Navajo Nation.
Description: Santa Fe : Sunstone Press, [2024] | Summary: "Indigenous tribes in Colorado survival was threatened by the discovery of gold, squatters lust for farming and ranching land and a push for the removal of all Indians"-- Provided by publisher.
Identifiers: LCCN 2024013644 | ISBN 9781632936714 (paperback) | ISBN 9781632936721 (hardback) | ISBN 9781611397444 (epub)
Subjects: LCSH: Indians of North America--Colorado--Government relations. | Indians of North America--Colorado--History--19th century. | Cultural property--Destruction and pillage--Colorado.
Classification: LCC E78.C6 H37 2024 | DDC 978.8/00497--dc23/eng/20240405
LC record available at https://lccn.loc.gov/2024013644

WWW.SUNSTONEPRESS.COM
SUNSTONE PRESS / POST OFFICE BOX 2321 / SANTA FE, NM 87504-2321 /USA
(505) 988-4418

DEDICATION

For My Beloved Brothers, Pat and Peter.

They were badly beaten by officials within the public school system, day-after-day, because they were Indian and wouldn't give in to them. I was a child and there was nothing I thought I could do to stop them. My parents did not know how to approach the school system. My brothers dropped out of school at an early age. It still hurts me very badly that my beloved brothers were cruelly abused because they were Indian.

ACKNOWLEDGMENTS

My Family

Nobody has been more helpful to me in the pursuit of this project than the members of my family for whom I am so very thankful. I could not have the time for research and writing without their active support. They encouraged me and made sure that whatever resources I needed for this project were available: computer, printer, supplies, etc. Thank you to my most beloved husband (who made breakfast, lunch and dinner and took over all daily family responsibilities so I could focus on this project) whose love provides such joy and stability in my life.

CONTENTS

Preface ~ 19
Indians in Colorado Pre-Contact ~ 21
Ute Bands ~ 21
Contact with Spain ~ 22
Mexican Land Grants ~ 23
U.S. Military Expeditions ~ 24
1849: Treaty of Abiquiú—U.S. Jurisdiction Over Capote and Muache Bands, Safe Passage for Settlers, Presence of Military Forts and Trading Posts—No Cession of Lands
U.S. Indian Treaties ~ 27
1851: Treaty of Fort Laramie—Safe Passage for Settlers, Presence of Military Forts ~ 28
1853: Commissioner: Cheyenne, Arapaho
 and Western Sioux Starving ~ 29
1854–1855: Military Campaign against Utes ~ 29
U.S. Indian Agencies in Colorado ~ 30
 Upper Arkansas Indian Agency ~ 31
 Conejos Indian Agency (Utes) ~ 31
 Middle Park Indian Agency (Utes) ~ 32
 Denver Special Indian Agency (Utes) ~ 32
 Los Piños Indian Agency (Utes) ~ 33
 White River Ute Agency (Utes) ~ 33
1857: Denver City Promoters ~ 33
1858: Discovery of Gold in Colorado ~ 33
1859: Clear Creek Gold Discovery ~ 34
1859: Miners' Court ~ 34
1859: Colorado Mineral Belt, Domain of Arapaho,

Cheyenne and Ute ~ 34
1859: Upper Platte, Agent Twiss, Diminution of Game ~ 35
1859: Upper Arkansas Agency, Superintendent Bent, Encroachments of Whites on Indian Lands ~ 36
1859: Commissioner Report to Secretary Interior, Critical State ~ 37
1860: Whites in Colorado Gold Region in Violation of Federal Law ~ 37
1861: Treaty of Fort Wise, Confine Cheyenne and Arapaho on Reservation, 1/13 Size of Fort Laramie Treaty Lands ~ 38
'Squatters' ~ 40
1861: Colorado Established as Territory ~ 40
1861: Colley Appointed Indian Agent for Upper Arkansas Indian Agency ~ 41
1861: Commissioner—Difficult to Manage Indian Affairs due to Lack of Treaties ~ 41
1861: 1st Regiment Colorado Volunteer Infantry Organized ~ 41
1862: Colorado Territorial Delegate—Miners Overrunning Ute Lands ~ 41
1862: Middle Park Agency Established for Utes ~ 42
1862: Commissioner Dole: Colorado and WASH Gold Rushes Infringing on Indian Rights ~ 43
March 1863: Delegation of Cheyenne, Arapaho, Comanche, Kiowa and Caddo Chiefs Visit Washington, DC—Dissuade Them from Joining Confederacy ~ 43
1863: Commissioner Dole to Governor/Superintendent Evans—Get Cheyenne and Arapaho that Have Not Signed Treaty of Fort Wise to Do So ~ 44
August 1863: Governor/Superintendent Evans Council with Cheyenne and Arapaho Leaders, Big Timbers ~ 44
October 1863: Commissioner Dole Confirms Mineral Wealth of Colorado Territory ~ 45
October 1863: Treaty of Conejos Only with Tabeguache Utes—Cede Land East of Continental Divide and Middle Park ~ 45
November 1863: Letter from Governor Evans to Commissioner Dole regarding Indian State of War ~ 46
April–May 1864: Colorado Volunteer Forces Make Unprovoked Attacks on Cheyenne Villages in Colorado Territory ~ 47
April 12, 1864: Battle of Fremont's Orchard, Colorado Volunteer Cavalry and Cheyenne, NE/Colorado ~ 48

May 3, 1864: Without Provocation, Colorado Volunteer Cavalry Attacks Peaceful Cheyenne Leaders at Cedar Bluffs, Kansas - 48
May 31, 1864: Letter to Major Wynkoop from Colonel John Chivington, Whip Cheyennes - 49
June 1, 1864: Mystery of Hungate Family -49
1864: Four Colorado Forts - 50
June 3, 11, 13, 1864: Governor Evans Demands Federal Troops Be Sent to Denver - 51
June 14, 1864: Governor Evans Wires Secretary of War to Muster Colorado Volunteer Cavalry into U.S. Service - 52
June 15, 1864: Major McKenny Warns General Curtis that Colorado's Volunteer Cavalry May Start Plains Indian War - 53
June 27, 1864: First Proclamation, Governor Evans, Colorado Superintendency Indian Affairs, Denver - 54
August 10, 1864: Governor Evans Requests 10,000 U.S. Troops from Secretary of War; Requests Commissioner Dole to Lobby for His Troops Request - 55
August 11, 1864: Governor Evans Proclamation to Citizens of Colorado Authorizing Them to Kill Hostile Indians - 55
Analysis of Governor Evans' Second Proclamation of August 11, 1864—University of Denver's John Evans Study Committee - 57
August 12, 1864: 3rd Regiment Authorized for 100 Days - 58
August 18, 1864: Governor Evans Sends Letter to Secretary of War that Colorado Is in Danger of Destruction from Indians - 58
August 19, 1864: Secretary of War Informs Governor Evans, due to Civil War, Shortage of U.S. Army Troops - 59
August 29, 1864: Chief Black Kettle and Other Chiefs Have Letters Sent to Agent Colley and Major Wynkoop Seeking Peace Talks - 59
Sep. 4-18, 1864: Chief Black Kettle Letter, Peace Talk Request Delivered to Major Wynkoop; Major Wynkoop Meets with Black Kettle at Smoky Hill River and Confirms Cheyenne and Arapaho Seeking Peace; Wynkoop Agrees to Escort Cheyenne and Arapaho Chiefs to Meet with Governor Evans regarding Peace - 59
Sep. 4, 1864: Governor Evans Informed by Agent Colley that Cheyenne and Arapaho Desire Peace - 60
Sep. 14, 1864: Governor Evans Forwards Agent Colley's Letter that Cheyenne and Arapaho Desire Peace to Colonel Chivington - 60
Sep. 18, 1864: Major Wynkoop Reports Meeting with Cheyenne and

Arapaho regarding Peace to Acting Assistant Adjutant-General, District of Upper Arkansas ~ 61

Sep. 28, 1864: Governor Evans Meets with Cheyenne and Arapaho Peace Party; Rejects Peace Offer Alleging State of War with
    Military in Control ~ 62

Sep. 29, 1864: Governor Evans Sends False Letter to Major Curtis, U.S. Army, that Sioux Plan to Attack Colorado ~ 63

Sep. 29, 1864: Governor Evans Sends Letter to Agent Colley regarding Meeting with Cheyenne and Arapaho Peace Party; That He Rejected Peace Offer due to U.S. State of War ~ 63

Sep. 29, 1864: Governor Evans Forwards Letter from Agent Colley to Colonel Chivington that Cheyenne and Arapaho Peace Offer
    Denied ~ 64

October 14, 1864: Colonel Chivington Orders Captain Nichols, Colorado Third Regiment, to Kill All Indians He Encounters ~ 65

October 15, 1864: Commissioner Dole Orders Governor Evans to Negotiate for Peace with Indians when They Offer, Regardless of U.S. State of War ~ 65

November 4, 1864: Major Wynkoop Relieved of Command ~ 65

November 15, 1864: Majors Anthony and Wynkoop Meet with Cheyenne and Arapaho Who Continue to Press for Peace ~ 66

November 15, 1864: Commissioner Dole Reports to Secretary of Interior that Cheyenne and Arapaho Urge Peace ~ 67

November 16, 1864: Major Anthony Reports to Headquarters that Cheyenne and Arapaho Appealing for Peace ~ 67

November 28, 1864: Major Anthony Reports Arrival of Colorado Third Regiment at Fort Lyon—1000 Soldiers ~ 67

November 28, 1864: Major General Curtis Reports to Brigadier General Carleton that Cheyenne and Arapaho Are Begging for Peace ~ 68

November 29, 1864: Sand Creek Massacre—Colonel Chivington Reports Killing 400-500 Indians; Scalped Every Man, Woman and Child, Mutilated Their Bodies; Removed Private Parts as War Trophies ~ 68

Report on Sand Creek Massacre by Indian Agent Leavenworth ~ 69

Sand Creek Massacre Reported as "Disastrous and Shameful
    Occurance" ~ 70

December 7, 1864: Colonel Chivington's Second Report to Governor Evans: Killed 500 Indians, Still in Pursuit of Cheyenne and Arapaho ~ 71

December 15, 1864: Major Anthony Reports Sand Creek Massacre Was

Terrible; Should Be Done to All Hostile Tribes ~ 71
Governor Evans Culpability in Sand Creek Massacre—University of Denver's John Evans Study Committee ~ 71
January 16, 1865: Sand Creek Military Investigation ~ 72
1865: U.S. Condemns Sand Creek Massacre ~ 73
April 28, 1865: Treaty with Arapaho and Cheyenne for Colorado Land, Offer No Money, No Specific Land for New Reservation ~ 73
1865: Superintendent Taylor, Upper Platte; Obstruction of Mining Prejudicial to U.S. ~ 74
October 11-13, 1865: U.S. Treaty Delegation, Arapaho and Cheyenne Still Recovering from Sand Creek, Not Ready to Agree to Relinquish Land in Colorado ~ 74
October 13, 1865: Treaty Council with Arapaho and Cheyenne—Unfortunately for You, Gold Discovered in Your Country ~ 75
October 14, 1865: Cheyenne and Arapaho Treaty Signed Removing Them from Colorado ~ 76
Little Arkansas Treaty—Land Specified for Reservation for Arapaho and Cheyenne in Indian Territory Already Given to Another Tribe ~ 76
January 1–February 2, 1865: Indian Military Campaign ~ 77
1865: Battle of Fort Rankin ~ 78
1866: Governor Evans' Speech on Minerals, Agriculture Promoting Colorado ~ 79
1866: Gold, Silver and Coal Discovered on Ute Land; Fertile Land, Timber, Water Power, All Requirements for Profitable Occupation ~ 80
1867: American Express Co., Shoot Indians ~ 81
1867: Central City Indian Scalp Bounty ~ 81
1867: Medicine Lodge Treaties—Cheyenne and Arapaho Treaty Establishing Reservation in Indian Territory ~ 82
1868: Battle of Beecher Island ~ 83
1868: Ute Treaty of 1868—Utes Cede Central Rockies ~ 83
1869: Battle at Summit Springs ~ 84
1871: Indian Appropriations Act Ends Treaty-Making with Indian Nations ~ 86
1872: Colorado Citizens Want 1868 Treaty Revised for Utes to Cede San Juan Mts. due to Silver Discoveries ~ 87
1873: San Juan Mountains—Richest Mining District ~ 88
1874: Brunot Agreement—Utes Cede Mineral Rich
    San Juan Mountains ~ 88

1876: Colorado Statehood ~ 88
1877: Stay Friendly with Utes ~ 89
1877: Comanche Peace Treaty with Utes ~ 89
1877: Commissioner Recommends Removing All Indians in Colorado and AZ to Indian Territory to Facilitate Mining and Farming by Whites
Colorado Petitions for Removal of All Utes ~ 90
1879: Battle of Milk Creek and Meeker Incident—Through No Fault, Utes Forced out of Colorado ~ 91
Sample News Headlines from Colorado Rocky Mountain News (1878–79) ~ 93
October 1879: Leadville Chronicle ~ 94
1879: Governor Pitkin's Order: Bring in, Dead or Alive, All Hostile Indians ~ 94
1880: Cong. Investigation—Battle of Milk Creek ~ 95
1880: General Pope—Utes Worthless ~ 97
Commissioner in Favor of Utes Removal to Utah ~ 97
1880: After Thornburgh/Meeker Incidents Ute Delegation Forced to DC to Punish Them by Dispossessing Them of Their Reservation ~ 97
1880: Utes Bribed to Sign Agreement to Cede Colorado Lands ~ 98
1880–1881: Commission Removes Utes ~ 99
1881: Forced Military Removal of 200 Miles ~ 99
1881: Whites Pour onto Land Left by Utes with No Shred of Common Decency ~ 99
1881: Cattle Enterprises ~ 100
1881: Legislative Assembly of Colorado Territory: Bill for an Act to provide for the Destruction of Indians and Skunks ~ 100
1890: Commissioner Morgan—Southern Utes to Stay in Colorado ~ 101
1895: Hunter Act—Opened Up Ute Strip to Homesteading and Sale ~ 102
1906: Mesa Verde Carved Out of Southern Ute Lands ~ 102
Colorado Moguls: Mining and Real Estate ~ 103
Metal Processing Enterprises ~ 104
City Developers, Denver, Colorado ~ 105
City Developers, Durango, Colorado ~ 106
Investment Banking ~ 106
Colorado Gold Production History ~ 107
Colorado's Mining Millionaires ~ 109
Colorado Counties ~ 114

"A Book of Christian History Bound in the Flayed Skin of an American Indian" ~ 115
Lenape Indians ~ 115
Disturbing Content ~ 115
John Wesley Iliff, Cattle Baron ~ 116
Wyoming's Cattle Industry Includes Iliff ~ 116
Colorado's Cattle Enterprises Includes Iliff ~ 117
1934 Rocky Mountain News Article: "An Indian Warrior's Skin, Finer Than the Finest Vellum, Forms The Binding Of An Ancient Book, *The History Of Christianity*, One Of The Most Treasured Relics In The Library Of The Iliff School Of Theology" ~ 118
Mid-1970s: Three White Iliff Students Concerned about Book Repatriation Proceedings ~ 119
Book Cover Turned over to American Indian Movement ~ 119
Confidentiality Broken by Prof. George "Tink" Tinker, an Osage Scholar Hired by Iliff in 1985 ~ 120
Iliff President Tom Wolfe Collaborates with Prof. Tinker on Course to Follow ~ 120
Interpretive Center at Iliff ~ 123
Iliff Agreed to Relationship with Lenape People ~ 123
President Wolfe's Goal regarding Iliff's Commitment to Lenape People Going Forward ~ 124
Rev. Wolfe, 2023 IAMSCU Flame of Excellence Award for His Contribution While President at Iliff (2013-2023) ~ 125
Appendix ~ 126
Notes ~ 130

PREFACE

In 1776, the Dominguez and Escalante Expedition explored and mapped the region from Santa Fe, New Mexico to as far north as today's Dinosaur National Monument in Colorado to the Uintah Valley and Salt Lake in Utah and across northeastern Arizona. Renowned cartographer, Don Bernardo Miera y Pacheco's map is crucial in understanding the extent of the land inhabited by various Ute Bands ("Yutahs") and the Arapaho ("Rapahu") in western Colorado. The Dominguez and Escalante Expedition, National Park Service, Map: https://www.nps.gov/dino/learn/historyculture/the-dominguez-and-escalante-expedition.htm (accessed online January 21, 2024). Escalante's route reads like a travel guide to the West: Santa Fe, Bandelier National Monument, Capulin National Monument, Arches National Monument, Wheeler National Monument, Mesa Verde National Park, Aztec Ruins, Yucca House, Hovenweep National Monuments, Natural Bridges National Monument, Colorado National Monument, Dinosaur National Monument, Timpanogos Cave National Monument, Cedar Breaks National Monument, Bryce Canyon National Park, Zion National Park, Pipe Springs National Monument, Grand Canyon National Park, Rainbow Bridge National Monument, Glen Canyon, Rainbow Lodge, Wupatki National Monument, Walnut Canyon National Monument, Montezuma's Castle, the Hopi Pueblos, Canyon de Chelly National Monument, Petrified Forest National Park, Zuni, Chaco Canyon National Monument, El Morro National Monument, Acoma Pueblo, Laguna, Isleta, and the Tiguex Pueblos. Russon, Robert S., "A Trail Guide to the Dominguez-Velez de Escalante Expedition 1776" (1973).

Primary Source Reliance

The author's reliance on numerous direct citations from relevant historical documents is to provide factual evidence of the subject. This format derives from her view that the material under discussion here is best experienced by the contemporaneous voice unfiltered by time or latter-day interpretations and revisions.

Different Names for a Particular Tribe

American Indian people describe their own cultures and the places they come from in many ways. Tribes often have more than one name. When Europeans arrived in the Americas, they used inaccurate pronunciations of the tribal names or used a name that another tribe used to refer to that tribe or renamed the tribes with European names.

Different Names for Land Areas in "America"

The competition between Spain, France, Great Britain and the U.S. to establish "sovereignty" over lands inhabited by Indian peoples led to a variety of names for the same areas and 'alleged' jurisdiction over them.

European Names for Indigenous Areas

Spain, France, the British and the U.S. all had names for indigenous areas as well. The U.S. would establish large Territories which would then be reduced in size to smaller territories and then become states, with modification of state lines as well.

Personal Names; Spelling

The names of historical American Indian people can cause much confusion for historians and readers. People often received several names over the course of their lives. A single person might have a birth name, a clan name, a name related to a good deed or act of bravery, and a French, Spanish, or English name used by Europeans or Americans. A tribal name could be spelled in numerous different ways.

Spelling Differed; Quotes Use Original Text

Spelling of words differed also. In this book, quotes used reflect original text, which may have different spellings, punctuation or mis-spellings or mis-punctuation. Please keep this in mind while reading this material.

Indians in Colorado Pre-Contact

Prior to the Europeans, the Ute were centered in the mountains and canyonlands, and the Arapaho and Cheyenne on the Great Plains. The hunting or wintering sites overlapped along the Front Range of the Rocky Mountains. Comanche and Kiowa also lived and hunted within the present boundaries of the state.

Within the Ute tribe there were subdivisions including Uncompahgre, Weeminuche, Muache, Capote, and others. These subdivisions related primarily to geographic locations and not major cultural differences. The Ute expanded to the point that by the time Europeans came into their land, they ranged from Pike's Peak on the east to the Great Salt Lake on the west, and from Taos in the south, to Wyoming's Green River country on the north.[1]

In 1840, the Kiowa, Comanche, and Lakota joined the Cheyenne and Arapaho in an unprecedented alliance to resolve territorial disputes and counter the growing number of emigrants headed west.

Ute Bands

The largest of the Ute Bands lived in west-central Colorado along the Gunnison and Uncompahgre river valleys. These were the Tabeguache (Taviwatch) or Uncompahgre Utes. North of them the Parianuche (Parusanuch), or Grand Valley Utes, lived along the Colorado River. The Yampa River Valley was home to the Yampa band, which also occupied North and Middle Parks. When the White River Agency was established in Meeker, the Grand Valley and Yampa bands came to be known as the White River Utes. In the Uintah Basin near today's Dinosaur National Monument in northeastern Utah and northwestern Colorado, were the Uintah Utes. The Tabeguache, White River, and Uintah bands together are now known as the Northern Utes. For the next 20 years there was constant pressure on the Utes to relinquish their land by the U.S., the State of Colorado, and mining and railroad interests. This was done by a series of negotiations and treaties entered into by the U.S.

Contact with Spain

In 1595, the viceroy of New Mexico selected Juan de Oñate y Salazar to lead an expedition of northern New Spain in search of gold. Oñate began the expedition in Jan. 1598 with 400 settlers, soldiers, and livestock. The expedition crossed the Rio Grande at present-day El Paso, Texas, and on April 30, 1598, he claimed all of New Mexico for King Phillip II of Spain, including what is today southern Colorado. That summer, his party established the colony of New Mexico for Spain and became New Mexico's first governor. Hearing about plentiful game to the north in the San Luis Valley, Oñate sent an expedition there to hunt bison. The party came across a village of about fifty Ute lodges; the Utes greeted them warmly, and some of the Ute men volunteered to help the inexperienced Spaniards hunt bison. Their relations with the Utes remained friendly until the 1630s, when Spaniards attacked a band and took about eighty Utes as slaves. Thereafter, Utes began raiding Spanish parties and communities for livestock and goods.

During the seventeenth and eighteenth centuries, the San Luis Valley remained largely indigenous, barely even a remote outpost of the Spanish Empire. Comanche raids on New Mexican communities increased during the eighteenth century.

In 1776, the Dominguez and Escalante Expedition, explored and mapped the region from Santa Fe, New Mexico to as far north as today's Dinosaur National Monument in Colorado to the Uintah Valley and Salt Lake in Utah and across northeastern Arizona. The Franciscan Friars Atanasio Domínguez and Silvestre Vélez de Escalante were searching for a route to the missions in Monterrey, CA. They encountered the Utes (Yutahs) who provided two guides who they named "Silvestre," and "Joaquin," a 12 year old boy who helped guide the party through its entire journey. They traveled and headed west to the Uintah Valley where they reached Salt Lake. Another 12 year old guide from the Timpanagos who they named

Jose Maria helped them out from near Provo to Cedar City. With winter approaching, they drew lots to decide whether to continue on or return to Santa Fe. They chose to return to Santa Fe, but without a guide they lost a significant amount of time finding a site to ford the Colorado River.

Their prolific and renowned cartographer, Don Bernardo Miera y Pacheco, was a retired military engineer who lived in Santa Fe. He had earlier mapped "Nuevo Mexico" which described the entire province, its twenty-two pueblos, population statistics, livestock numbers, and men and military equipment available for defense. His map is crucial in understanding the extent of the land inhabited by various Ute Bands ("Yutahs") and the Arapaho ("Rapahu") in western Colorado. Traveling into Utah, he mapped the Timpanogos who lived in the Utah and Salt Lake Valleys and "indios barbones" - bearded Indians in central Utah. Traveling south into Arizona, he mapped the region inhabited by the Havasupai ("Cosninas") and the Hopis ("Moquinos"). Coming back into New Mexico, he mapped the Pueblos of Zuni and Acoma. His legendary map opened up the region to future exploration and trade.

In 1779, the Spanish war party of Juan Bautista de Anza picked up Ute and Jicarilla Apache warriors on its way to fight the Comanche leader Cuerno Verde who had been raiding villages in northern New Mexico. With 800 men and 2,500 horses, de Anza led an expedition from New Mexico through Colorado and across the Arkansas River to engage the Comanches. Cornering the chief near Rye, Colorado, the campaign killed him and several other headmen, which eventually precipitated the longest-lasting peace treaty ever signed by the Comanche with any of the governments of Spain, Mexico, or the U.S.

Colorado's first permanent settlers were citizens of Spain who made homes along the southern edges of Colorado settling in the San Luis Valley.

Mexican Land Grants

After winning independence from Spain in 1821, Mexico issued land grants in present-day New Mexico and Colorado to encourage settlement as a bulwark against rising American influence in the Southwest. In 1833, the Mexican government awarded the Conejos Grant, roughly spanning land between the Rio Grande and Conejos Creek near present-day Alamosa, to fifty families. In 1841, Mexico gave the Canadian trader Charles Beaubien and Mexican official Guadalupe Miranda the contested Maxwell Grant. In 1843-44, the Luis Maria Baca Grant No. 4 and the Sangre de Cristo Grant were granted in south-central Colorado (present-day Costilla County).

U.S. Military Expeditions

The U.S. Military Expeditions were part of the contested struggle for possession of the west. A large part of this vast domain was claimed by Spain and, thereafter, Mexico. Part of the expeditions included gathering intelligence on Spain's control of the southwest, which the U.S. might challenge. The U.S. knew Spain was too weak to go to war to defend its 'discovery' claim in the southwest.

When France sold Louisiana to the U.S. in 1803 it conveyed: "forever and in full Sovereignty the said territory [Louisiana] with all its rights and appurtenances as fully and in the Same manner as they have been acquired by the French Republic in virtue of the above mentioned Treaty concluded with his Catholic Majesty." (Treaty of San Ildefonso, 1800). France's Foreign Minister Talleyrand was deliberately vague and unhelpful about the boundaries: "You must take it as we received it."[2] Congress approved the purchase on Oct. 31, 1803, and the U.S. took possession on Dec. 20, 1803.

After the Purchase, President Jefferson wanted to claim as much territory as possible given the vague description of the boundaries. There was limited geographical knowledge of North America, as well as confusion resulting from the competing territorial claims of the European powers. In an 1803 Letter, Jefferson claimed land on the west to the Rio Norte or Bravo.

From Thomas Jefferson to Thomas Paine, Monticello, Aug. 10, 1803

> The unquestioned extent of Louisania [sic] on the sea is from the Iberville to the Mexicana River, or perhaps the high lands dividing that from the Missisipi [sic]. it's original boundary however as determined by occupation of the French was Eastwardly to the river Perdido (between Mobile & Pensacola) & Westward to the Rio Norte or Bravo.[3]

In 1805, U.S. Army General James Wilkinson ordered Lieutenant Zebulon Pike to lead 20 soldiers on a reconnaissance of the upper Mississippi River. On a second expedition in 1806-1807, Pike ultimately explored the west and southwest, including today's Kansas, Colorado, New Mexico, Texas and Louisiana. Most importantly, Pike was to ascertain what the Spanish were doing along the uncertain southwestern border of the Louisiana Territory. A letter between Pike and Wilkinson, written on July 22, 1806, directed Pike to scout as close as possible to Santa Fe, allowing for the possibility that he might be captured by Spanish authorities. If discovered, he would use the cover story that he had become lost while en route to Natchitoches, Louisiana. On Feb. 26, 1807, a troop of Spanish soldiers rode up to Pike's stockade and informed him that he was in Spanish territory. The Spanish patrol rounded up the frostbitten stragglers, escorting the entire party to Santa Fe. Pike's papers were confiscated, and he was sent south to Chihuahua. Neither Pike nor his men were mistreated; the majority were returned to the U.S. at Natchitoches on June 30, 1807. The Spanish Governor was reprimanded by his King for releasing Pike before receiving an apology from the U.S. for trespassing.

Major Stephen Long's 1819-1820 expedition mapped the central Plains to the Rocky Mountains. Long was the first Army explorer to include professional scientists on his survey team. He also was the first to use a steamboat for exploration purposes. Setting out from Council Bluffs, he crossed the plains to Colorado, explored the Front Range of Colorado, and then followed the Rocky Mountain Front down into New Mexico.

The orders regarding these military expeditions included gathering detailed intelligence, not only on Spain, and thereafter, Mexico, but on the number, strength, allies and military capacity of Indians should the U.S. continue its westward expansion.

Zebulon Pike: 1805-06; 1806-07; Upper reaches of the Mississippi; the southwest. Pike's Peak; explored much of the Mississippi's upper regions.

Stephen A. Long: 1819-20; Plains along the Platte River to the Colorado Rockies. Explored and named Long's Peak; measured the height of Pike's Peak; collected plant, rock, and animal specimens for public viewing; provided more accurate maps.

John C. Fremont: 1842; Plains up the Platte River to Fort Laramie to the South Pass gateway to Oregon to the Wind River Range. Removed the label of "Great American Desert" from the plains which provided for farming and supplies for emigrants.

James W. Abert and Thomas Fitzpatrick: 1845-46; New Mexico, Oklahoma, Texas. Mapped locations of water, wood, and grass; information on Comanche and Kiowa; described Rio Grande Valley, its uses, and possibilities for region.

William H. Emory: 1846; New Mexico, California. Provided intelligence that NM would require irrigation, scarce fertile lands that would make slavery unprofitable; Mexican government not responsive to citizens, therefore there would be little local resistance to American roads or railroads; first accurate maps of Southwest.

1849 - Treaty of Abiquiú - U.S. Jurisdiction Over Capote and Muache Ute Bands, Safe Passage for Settlers, Presence of Military Forts and Trading Posts - No Cession of Lands

The Utes initially benefited from the fact that the large immigrant trails and the transcontinental railroad skirted their mountain home but it didn't last long. The one point of friction between the white and Ute cultures originated with the movement of settlers from New Mexico into the fertile San Luis Valley in south-central Colorado. In late Dec. 1849, in his capacity as Indian Agent, James Calhoun brought together Ute leaders—mostly from the Capote and Muache bands—and American officials at Abiquiú, a village along the Chama River in northern New Mexico.

The U.S. sought to pacify the Territory of New Mexico and the San Luis Valley which had been acquired as a result of the Mexican-American War. The U.S. sought free passage of American citizens through Ute territory, as well as the construction of "military posts," Indian agencies, and "trading houses" on Ute lands. In return, it promised to protect Utes against depredations by American citizens, as well as provide "such donations, presents, and implements" deemed necessary for the Utes to "support themselves by their own industry." These "donations" would come in the form of annuities—annual deliveries of food and supplies. The Treaty involved no cession of lands and did not set apart any reservation to the Indians, though it clearly recognized the rights of the Utes in the territory covered by the Treaty.

The resulting Treaty of Abiquiú (9 Stats., 984) was signed by twenty-eight leaders of the "Utah tribe of Indians," placing the Utes "lawfully and exclusively under the jurisdiction of the [U.S.] government" in "perpetual peace and amity."

The agency designated to provide the "donations" was in Taos which made securing the promised annuities difficult. The Treaty failed to give the Utes the reliable food supply they had sought through diplomacy. More importantly, it failed to protect the Indian lands from being overrun by whites and two more treaties would be demanded of the Utes to secure mineral resources.

This is an instance recognized by General John Pope regarding Indian treaties in his 1878 speech:

> The first demand by the Indians, as the principal condition of the treaty, is that the white man shall not intrude upon his reserved lands, nor destroy his game, nor interfere with his people. This condition is the first and most important to the Indian. In every case of which I know anything, it has been readily agreed to, and the government, through its commissioners, binds itself to this obligation. Is it possible that any white man, official or private citizen, believes that, even if the government intends to enter into this obligation in good faith, it is practicable to fulfill the engagement? What means has the government to enforce compliance?[4]

U.S. Indian Treaties

The high cost of military campaigns impressed upon the U.S. the need for negotiations with Indians. The Treaties entered into weren't for the benefit of the Indians - they were to satisfy the U.S.' Manifest Destiny Military Goal. From the time of George Washington, the goal of a continental empire from sea to sea was the overriding plan. The Indians were an impediment and would be dealt with initially by a three-prong strategy - (1) use settlers to achieve military objectives of seizing territory and exterminating or otherwise controlling Indians; (2) implement an administrative policy of forced removal with the aid of the military and private contractors; and (3) when more land was needed for emigrants enter into treaties of peace or treaties of cession of land.

1851 - Treaty of Fort Laramie - Safe Passage for Settlers, Presence of Military Forts

In 1834, during the height of the fur trade in the American West, American traders William Sublette and Robert Campbell established what became Fort Laramie in present-day Wyoming, at the confluence of the Laramie and North Platte Rivers. The Cheyenne, Arapaho, and Sioux often gathered there to trade bison robes for weapons, iron cookware, coffee, and other American goods. In the 1840s, increasing numbers of white migrants began traveling west to settle in the newly acquired territories of Oregon and California. Fort Laramie, then known as Fort John, became a popular waystation for migrants traveling the Great Platte River Road. Their wagon trains drove away game, trampled grazing grasses for bison, and consumed timber and other important resources on the Great Plains. This put the migrants in competition with the Cheyenne, Arapaho, and other local Indians.

In 1851, the U.S. invited all the Indian Nations of the northern Great Plains to gather for a treaty council at the mouth of Horse Creek, near Fort Laramie, where Nebraska and Wyoming now meet. The U.S.' purpose was to ensure a protected right-of-way for the emigrants crossing Indian lands and the establishment of military posts.

In attendance were: Oglala Sioux, Assiniboine, Arapaho, Shoshone (attended though not invited), Brule Sioux, Mandan, Crow, Arikara, Rees, Cheyenne, Gros Ventre, Hidatsa and Snake. The Comanche, Kiowa and Apache refused to attend.

It was the largest gathering of Plains Indian Nations in American history. More than ten thousand people (men, women and children) attended. The

Fort Laramie Treaty is also referred to as the Horse Creek Treaty since the treaty location had to be moved from the Fort due to insufficient forage for the thousands of horses.

The 1851 Treaty of Fort Laramie recognized the sovereignty and territories of the different signatory tribes who pledged an end to warfare and to live in peace with one another. To compensate for their diminishing subsistence base, the Nations were promised annuities, so long as white travelers were allowed free and unmolested travel across Colorado and the Army could build and man forts. Many of the emigrants were headed for California and Oregon.

Whereas the government promised to distribute $50,000 in annuities among all nine nations for fifty years, the U.S. Senate ratified the treaty, adding Article 5, which adjusted the compensation from fifty to ten years, if the tribes accepted the changes. All tribes accepted the change with the exception of the Crow.

Each nation then selected delegates to tour the eastern U.S.; these trips were designed to showcase the wealth and power of the U.S. so that Indian nations would abide by the treaty.[5]

The government's failure to deliver the promised annuities undercut the Treaty's two fundamental goals: to preserve peace between Indian nations and between Indians and whites. As their food sources diminished and government annuities failed to supplement the loss, the Indian nations fought each other for the best hunting grounds and attacked settlers intruding upon their lands.

1853 - Cheyenne, Arapaho and Western Sioux Starving

In 1853, Thomas Fitzpatrick, Indian Agent, Upper Platte and Arkansas, reported that the Cheyenne, Arapaho, and western Sioux were "in a starving state ... Their women are pinched with want, and their children constantly crying out with hunger."[6]

1854-1855 - Military Campaign against Utes

On Dec. 25, 1854, a small band of Mouache Utes, under the leadership of Tierra Blanca, killed four trappers. The Army gathered a force of twelve companies of Regulars and militia at Fort Garland to pursue the Utes but quickly came to the conclusion that winter was not the best season for active campaigning in the Rockies. The size of the Army force, however, impressed the Utes, who had avoided contact with the troops by melting away into the mountains. A peace was negotiated in the fall of 1855.

U.S. Indian Agencies in Colorado

The federal regulation of Indian affairs in the U.S. first included development of the position of Indian agent in 1793 under the Second Trade and Intercourse Act. The legislation also authorized the President to "appoint such persons, from time to time, as temporary agents to reside among the Indians," and guide them into acculturation of American society by developing agricultural practices and domestic activities. Eventually, the U.S. ceased using the word "temporary" in the Indian agent's job title.

The two principal types of field jurisdictions of the Office of Indian Affairs in the 19th century were superintendencies and agencies, which would come into play in Colorado. Superintendents of Indian Affairs for a specific locality existed from approximately 1803 until 1878, when the last Superintendency was abolished. A Superintendent of Indian Affairs was an administrator whose duties included the supervision of relations between the tribes and non-Indians, the supervision of the conduct and accounts of agents responsible to them, the communication of instructions from the Commissioner to agents, and the granting of leaves of absence to subordinates. It was also common practice for them to receive contract bids, enter into contracts, and issue annuities to the Indians. Under each superintendent were agents, subagents, or special agents immediately responsible for one or more tribes. The records of the Superintendencies evidence the broad areas of responsibility including documents relating to negotiation and enforcement of treaties; land surveys and allotments; Indian removal; annuity and other payments; Indian delegations; intrusions on Indian lands; traders and licenses; enforcement of federal laws and regulations; hostilities and military operations; depredation claims; location of agencies; school attendance and curricula; medical treatment; production at blacksmith, gunsmith, and wheelwright shops;

construction and repair of buildings; and purchase and transportation of goods and supplies.

The St. Louis Superintendency was established in 1822 and was responsible for the agencies located in the Midwest, including Colorado. It operated until 1851, when it was succeeded by the Central Superintendency. The Central Superintendency was originally responsible for most of the Indians in what is now Kansas and Nebraska, and in the upper regions of the Missouri, Platte, and Arkansas Rivers in the Dakotas, Wyoming, and Colorado. The agencies assigned to the Central Superintendency included the Upper Platte, Upper Missouri, Upper Arkansas, Ponca, and Yankton agencies. The Colorado Superintendency of Indian Affairs was not established until 1861 when Colorado received Territorial status. The Territorial Governor served as the ex officio Superintendent of Indian Affairs. John Evans assumed that position on May 16, 1862.

The Tabeguache and Muache Utes were attached to the Taos Agency in northern New Mexico under the jurisdiction of Kit Carson by 1856. Despite being administered by the Taos Agency, the Tabeguache Utes resided in western and south-central Colorado, including the Uncompahgre and San Luis Valleys. The Muache band roamed farther south and was more closely attached to the Taos Agency.

The Indian agencies in Colorado were as follows:

Upper Arkansas Indian Agency

The Upper Arkansas Indian Agency was established in 1855 at Bent's New Fort to superintend Nations along the upper part of the Arkansas River in eastern Colorado and western Kansas. The original agency was assigned to the Central Superintendency and was under its supervision until the establishment of the Colorado Superintendency in 1861. In 1866 the agency moved to Kansas.[7]

Conejos Indian Agency (Utes)

Annuity goods—annual payments made to Indians as stipulated by treaties—for the Tabeguache and Muache Utes were distributed at

Conejos in the San Luis Valley beginning in 1858. For convenience, the goods were stored and distributed at Lafayette Head's ranch at Conejos in 1859. In order to more effectively administer the Tabeguache Utes, the Conejos Agency was established in 1860 at Head's Ranch, and Head was appointed Indian agent. After the Treaty of 1868 established a reservation for the Utes west of the Rocky Mountains, a new agency was established in 1869 on the reservation and the Conejos Agency was abandoned.

Middle Park Indian Agency (Utes)

The Middle Park Agency was established in 1862 for the Grand River, Uinta, and Yampa Utes. After the Treaty of 1868 established a reservation for the Utes west of the Rocky Mountains in Colorado, the agency was moved to a location on the White River in 1869 and became known as the White River Agency.

Denver Special Indian Agency (Utes)

To deal with the large number of Utes off the reservation, the Board of Indian Commissioners appointed Robert Campbell and Felix R. Brunot to a committee to meet with Colorado Governor Edward M. McCook in 1870. They concluded that the best solution was to establish a special agency in Denver rather than create a conflict by forcing the Utes onto the reservation. These off-reservation Utes received their annuity goods - items promised to them by treaty in return for their land—at the Denver Agency. McCook's brother-in-law, James B. Thompson, began serving the Utes in Denver in 1869, when he arrived in Colorado as McCook's private secretary. On Jan. 17, 1871, Thompson was officially appointed the special agent for the Denver Agency; he also took over the administration of Indian affairs in Colorado from the Governor. The Agency served Utes who were accustomed to collecting supplies from Denver's Middle Park Agency during the 1860s, even though reassigned to a reservation west of the Rocky Mountains. It was decommissioned in Nov. 1874, but this did not prevent Utes from spending the winter in the Denver area. They still came to Denver expecting provisions, so the agency was reestablished and operational through 1875.

Los Piños Indian Agency (Utes)

Under provisions of the 1868 treaty, an agency was to be established by the Office of Indian Affairs on the Los Piños River in extreme southern Colorado to serve some of the Ute bands. For various reasons the agency could not be constructed on the river. Instead, it was established in the high mountains near Cochetopa Pass south of Gunnison, which was close to the eastern boundary of the new reservation. It could not be easily supplied and the surrounding land was unsuitable for growing crops. It was relocated in 1875 to the Uncompahgre Valley. It was abandoned in 1881 after the Utes were forcibly removed by the military to Utah in the fall of 1881.

White River Agency (Utes)

The White River Agency at Meeker, Colorado, was established at the same time as the first Los Piños Agency under provisions of the Treaty of 1868. The agency was intended to serve the White River Ute band as well as some of the other bands from northwestern Colorado. As the site of the Meeker Incident and the Battle of Milk Creek, the White River Agency was the focal point of important episodes of violence between Indians and whites that led to the removal of many Utes from the state. It was abandoned after the White River Utes were forced into Utah.

1857 - Denver City Promoters

Denver already had promoters in 1857. The Denver City Town Company was formed in 1858 with the following members: E. I. Stout, president; General William Larimer, E. E. Whitsitt, James Reed, J. H. Dudley, Charles Blake, Norman Welton, A. J. Williams, General John Clancy, Samuel Curtis, Ned Wynkoop, McGaa and Charles Nichols. Most of their names have been perpetuated in the names of Denver's prominent streets.[8]

1858 - Discovery of Gold in Colorado

The first publicized discovery of gold in Colorado was in 1858. Prospectors traveling west to California's Gold Rush panned small amounts of gold at Cherry Creek, the South Platte River, and Ralston Creek. William Green Russell and a team of prospectors traveled to the South Platte River the next year and discovered gold at the Little Dry Creek, which is credited with launching the Pikes Peak Gold Rush in 1859. The immediate rush to the Denver area resulted in important placer finds near Idaho Springs and Central City. Panning gold from stream and terrace gravels is called placer mining, derived from the Spanish word placer or "pleasure"—the gold is available at one's pleasure.

Gold and other ore deposits were mostly in a northeast-trending belt, known as the Colorado mineral belt. From near Boulder on the northeast this belt extended southwest to the San Juan Mountains and beyond. The Cripple Creek District, the largest gold producer in Colorado, and several minor districts lay southeast of the mineral belt.

1859 - Clear Creek Gold Discovery

In Jan. of 1859, the prospector George A. Jackson found the first substantial amount of gold in Colorado where Chicago Creek empties into Clear Creek in present day Idaho Springs.

1859 - Miners' Court

The first miners' court was created in the Gregory District of Gilpin County, in 1859. Subsequent courts followed the Gregory model. The Gold Hill District was organized by a mass convention on July 23, 1859. Boulder's town company was organized on Feb. 10, 1859.

1859 - Colorado Mineral Belt, Domain of Arapaho, Cheyenne and Ute

The gold discoveries in the Colorado mineral belt were made on Indian land. Without regard to their rights, prospectors, miners and mercantilists flooded onto their land. The year 1859 was a critical one for Colorado's Indians. Commissioner of Indian Affairs ("Com'r") Greenwood informed Secretary Thompson that the U.S. had essentially deprived the Indians living in or hunting and gathering or visiting spiritual sites in the Colorado area of any means of traditional subsistence.

A crisis has now, however, arrived in our relations with them. Since the discovery of gold in the vicinity of "Pike's Peak," the emigration has immensely increased; the Indians have been driven from their local haunts and hunting grounds, and the game so far killed off or dispersed, that it is now impossible for the Indians to obtain the necessary subsistence from that source. ***In fact, we have substantially taken possession of the country and deprived them of their accustomed means of support.*** ... They have also been brought to realize that a stern necessity is impending over them; that they cannot pursue their former mode of life, but must entirely change their habits, and, in fixed localities, look to the cultivation of the soil and the raising of stock for their future support. There is no alternative to providing for them in this manner but to exterminate them, which the dictates of justice and humanity alike forbid. They cannot remain as they are; for, if nothing is done for them, they must be subjected to starvation, or compelled to commence robbing and plundering for a subsistence. (Emphasis added).[9]

1859 - Upper Platte, Agent Twiss, Diminution of Game

On Aug. 16, 1859, Thomas S. Twiss, the U.S. Indian Agent for the Upper Platte, submitted his grave concerns of possible Indian hostilities due to the incursion of whites on their lands to the Superintendent of Indian Affairs. His report, regarding the Arapaho and Cheyenne, was "animated solely with a ***desire to prevent their utter extinction.***" (Emphasis added). His Report was brought to the attention of the Senate in response to a resolution they passed for an "estimate of the amounts that will be required to hold councils with certain Indians of the plains and in the State of Minnesota." It was referred to the Committee on Indian Affairs.[10]

Agent Twiss expressed the fears of the Indians regarding the diminution of game due to penetration of their hunting grounds by whites:

> The state of the Indian mind among the wild tribes is one of extreme suspicion in all matters relating to the preservation of game, their only means of subsistence; and when it disappears the Indian must perish. Hence it has happened that, in some parts of the prairie

country, the Indians have stopped white people, and even United States topographical parties, when they have endeavored to penetrate to their hunting grounds, and have turned them back, pretty roughly too, for fear that the buffalo would be destroyed or scared away, and never return again. According to Agent Twiss, the buffalo "no longer covers the valleys of the North Platte and its tributaries, and makes the prairie appear black, as formerly, as far as the eye could scan the horizon..."[11] A Sioux chief in council expressed his fear regarding the discovery of gold: "On the south fork of the Platte the white people are finding gold, and the Arapahoes and Cheyennes have no longer any hunting grounds. Our country has become very small, and, before our children are grown up, we shall have no more game."[12]

This emigration, according to Agent Twiss, had resulted in "a tendency to irritate, excite, and exasperate the Indian mind, and fill it with alarm and jealousy to such a degree that an interruption to our friendly relations with the wild tribes may occur at any moment."[13]

1859 - Upper Arkansas Agency, Superintendent Bent, Encroachments of Whites on Indian Lands

Agent Twiss' fears were confirmed by the renowned Agent Bent. He announced that the Cheyenne and Arapaho were willing to treat with the U.S., due to the influx of gold miners taking over choice Indian lands and emigration through their hunting grounds reducing their subsistence on game.

They ask for pay for the large district known to contain gold, and which is already occupied by the whites, who have established the county of Arapahoe and many towns. They further ask annuities in the future for such lands as they may cede and relinquish to the government. ...[14]

The Cheyenne and Arapaho demand for pay for the gold in the region was fully warranted based on Agent Bent's substantiation and confirmation:

> *The explorations of this season have established the existence of the precious metals in absolutely infinite abundance* and convenience of position. The concourse of whites is therefore constantly swelling,

and incapable of control or restraint by the government. This suggests the policy of promptly rescuing the Indians, and withdrawing them from contact with the whites ... (Emphasis added).[15]

In accord with Agent Twiss' report, Agent Bent warned of possible predatory attacks on whites by the Comanches:

> A smothered passion for revenge agitates these Indians, perpetually fomented by the failure of food, the encircling encroachments of the white population, and the exasperating sense of decay and impending extinction with which they are surrounded. ... A desperate war of starvation and extinction is therefore imminent and inevitable, unless prompt measures shall prevent it.[16]

1859 - Commissioner Report to Secretary of the Interior, Critical State

In Nov. 1859, Commissioner Greenwood, in his Report to the Secretary ("Sec.") of the Interior Jacob Thompson, compelled "special attention to the reports of Messrs. Twiss and Bent, the agents for the Indians within the upper Platte and Arkansas agencies, embracing Sioux, Cheyenne, Arapahoe, Comanche, Kioway, and a portion of the Apache Indians. There is evidently a very critical state of affairs existing within those agencies, and serious difficulties must soon occur, unless timely measures are adopted to avert them."[17]

1860 - Whites in Colorado Gold Region in Violation of Federal Law

Stephen A. Douglas pointed out on the Senate floor on May 16, 1860, that "every man in Pike's Peak is there in violation of law; every man of them has incurred the penalty of $1,000 fine and six months' imprisonment for going in violation of the Indian intercourse law, and claiming land which was under Indian title."[18]

Four memorials of residents at and near the eastern slope of the Rocky Mountains, praying for the extinguishment of the Indian title, a survey and sale of the public lands, the establishment of an assay office, and the erection of a new territory from contiguous portions of New Mexico, Utah, Kansas, and Nebraska, were communicated to President Lincoln. In an address by General O.O. Howard, he recounted Lincoln's support for the miners: "Tell the miners for me I shall promote their interests to the best of my ability because their prosperity is the prosperity of the nation, and we shall prove in a very few years that we are indeed the treasury of the world."[19]

Fort Wise

Fort Wise, established just west of Bent's New Fort in Colorado, was built in 1860 and named for Henry Wise, Governor of Virginia. That same year, the U.S. Army leased William Bent's New Trading Post, which consisted of 12 rooms surrounding a central courtyard. Bent's New Fort buildings were used as a commissary for the Fort and housed the Upper Arkansas Indian Agency. It served as an important military link on the Santa Fe Trail between Fort Leavenworth, Kansas, and Fort Union, New Mexico. In 1861, the U.S. changed the name of the Post to Fort Lyon in honor of General Nathaniel Lyon, killed at the Battle of Wilson's Creek, Missouri, on Aug. 10, 1861. Cooperating with detachments from Fort Larned, Kansas, and Fort Union, New Mexico, its troops escorted traffic along the upper reaches of the Mountain Branch of the Santa Fe Trail from the Arkansas River to Raton Pass.

1861 - Treaty of Fort Wise, Confine Cheyenne and Arapaho on Reservation, 1/13 Size of Fort Laramie Treaty Lands

Under the 1851 Treaty of Fort Laramie, there was no authority for settlers to settle or mine for gold on any of the Indians lands. The fifty thousand miners and traders who came to Colorado in 1859 alone *squatted* on the legal homelands of the Cheyenne and Arapaho. The influential lobby of the miners and mercantilists that settled in Denver pressured the U.S. to renegotiate the 1851 Treaty and redefine Cheyenne and Arapaho lands to allow for continued settlement of the gold-rich Rocky Mountains, without fear of violence.

To this end, the U.S. sent Commissioner Greenwood to Bent's New Fort in the fall of 1860 to negotiate a treaty. It was planned to cordon the Cheyenne and Arapaho onto a subdivided, roughly triangular reservation of 4 million acres in the area near Sand Creek (bounded by the Arkansas

River near the northern border of New Mexico and the Big Sandy Creek). However, only ten chiefs signed the treaty: six Cheyennes, including Black Kettle (Motevato), and four Arapahos. Cheyenne chief Black Kettle protested since under Cheyenne political doctrine all tribal and military leaders (most of whom were not in attendance) had to be consulted before the treaty could be consummated. Many would later say they did not understand the terms and had not intended to cede the lands granted them under the 1851 Fort Laramie Treaty, which encompassed over 44 million acres. The majority of the Cheyenne and Arapaho did not move to the Reservation which was one-thirteenth the size of their former territory. The Indian Office considered the Treaty of Fort Wise to be applicable only to those bands whose leaders had agreed to it. Historian Frank Hall in his 1895 History of Colorado concurred with the Indians that it was secured by "presents and mystification."

> A treaty made with the Cheyenne and Arapaho at Bent's Fort in 1860, procured the cession of their lands east of the mountains to the government. It was no sooner signed than regretted. *They had been persuaded to the point of affixing their names to the instrument which dispossessed them of their ancient heritage by the usual means, presents and mystification. The more the act was contemplated the more resolute they became to expel the settlers and regain what they had foolishly surrendered.* (Emphasis added).[20]

The Treaty was signed by President Lincoln on Feb. 15, 1861.

Younger Cheyenne and Arapaho, especially those in the Cheyenne Dog Soldiers and other warrior societies, refused to abide by the terms of the Treaty. For more than a decade after the Treaty, the Dog Soldiers and similar groups staged raids throughout eastern Colorado, plundering small stagecoach and later railroad station towns.

It was on that reservation, along Sand Creek in present-day Kiowa County, that Colonel John Chivington and the Third Colorado Volunteers slaughtered peaceful Cheyenne and Arapaho—mostly women, children, and the elderly—in 1864.

'Squatters'

Squatters were those that simply occupied vacant public domain lands or Indian lands, even if Indian title hadn't been extinguished, often making improvements, "and took their chances on confirming legal title at a later date." *The popular belief on the frontier was that squatters were doing a national service by clearing the land and extending the area of civilization.* Commissioner of Indian Affairs Lea's solution to the colonial settlers' illegal encroachment on Indian lands was to promote the removal of Indians 'purportedly' out of harm's way. If they did not willingly move, they would be placed under military control and the U.S. Army would assure their eviction.

Eric Kades in "The Dark Side of Efficiency: Johnson v. M'Intosh and the Expropriation of American Indian Lands." *University of Pennsylvania Law Review* (2000), stated:

> More distressing was the policy to use the squatters as 'hired guns,' a military force against the Indians. They were willing to vigorously protect their alleged land rights. *"Settlers presented the Indians with a large local militia that made the odds of a victorious attack so low that, realizing their weakness, the tribes sold out cheaply. However, opposed the common law tradition might be to squatters, these settlers played an important role in expropriating Indian lands at minimal cost."* (Emphasis added).

1861 - Colorado Established as Territory

On Feb. 28, 1861, Colorado was established as a Territory. John Evans was appointed as Governor and ex oficio Superintendent of Indian Affairs. The Territory was opened to white settlement, even though Indian title had not been fully extinguished. Many tribes continued to view the land as theirs. Territorial officials lost no time in establishing seventeen counties, all of which were on Indian land. On Nov. 1, 1861, the State of Colorado was divided into 17 counties. From northwest to southeast they were: Summit, Larimer, Weld, Boulder, Gilpin, Clear Creek, Arapahoe, Jefferson, Douglas, Lake, Park, El Paso, Fremont, Pueblo, Guadalupe (Conejos), Costilla, and Huerfano. There also was the Cheyenne and Arapaho reservation, abutting the eastern boundaries of El Paso and Pueblo Counties. Present-day Colorado is divided into 64 counties.

1861 - Colley Appointed Indian Agent for Upper Arkansas Indian Agency

On July 26, 1861, Samuel G. Colley was appointed as the Indian Agent for the Upper Arkansas Indian Agency. He served in that role from 1861 to 1865. Around that same time Colley's cousin, William P. Dole, was appointed the Commissioner, which provided an avenue for communication regarding Indian issues.

1861 - Commissioner - Difficult to Manage Indian Affairs due to Lack of Treaties

In late 1861, Commissioner William Dole reported the difficulties faced in the newly established Colorado Territory ("CO TER") due to the lack of treaties with the tribes:

> The recent discovery of gold within this Territory has drawn thither a rapid tide of emigration, which being precipitated amongst the tribes occupying the gold bearing regions of the Territory, thus mingling the white and red races, without any treaties contemplating so radical a change in their relations, has greatly increased the difficulties in the way of a successful administration of its Indian affairs.[21]

1861 - 1st Regiment Colorado Volunteer Infantry Organized

On Aug. 26, 1861, Territorial Governor Evans organized the 1st Regiment of Volunteer Infantry. John Chivington was commissioned as a Major.

1862 - CO TER Delegate - Miners Overrunning Ute Lands

In 1862, the Colorado Territorial delegate to Congress (Hiram Pitt Bennet) noted that the **miners were "entirely overrunning the hunting grounds of Ute Indians** ... taking out large quantities of gold, killing and driving out game," and that despite treaties conferring ostensible protection, the "demand for Ute land continued unabated." (Emphasis added).[22]

1862 - Middle Park Agency Established for Utes

The Middle Park Agency was established in 1862 for the Grand River, Uinta, and Yampa Utes. The Utes spent their summers hunting elk, mule deer, and other game in Middle Park before returning to their winter camp in present-day Glenwood Springs. In addition to hunting, they were proficient gatherers and took from the landscape a wide assortment of wild berries, roots, and plants, such as the versatile yucca plant. By the mid-seventeenth century the Utes had obtained horses via the Spanish. The animals greatly improved Ute mobility and changed Ute culture.

Historian Frank Hall in his 1895 History of Colorado vividly described Middle Park and the Utes attachment to it.

> The Middle Park was the favorite home and hunting ground of the northern Ute Indians. Prior to the invasion of the Park by white settlers, quadruped and other game abounded elk, deer, mountain sheep, antelope, buffalo and all varieties of bear, including grizzlies; grouse, sage hens, ducks, geese, turkeys, etc. ... It was, in reality, the best hunting range in all the mountain region. It is watered by Grand River, a large and noble stream, fed by many strong tributaries; a beautiful and picturesque basin well grassed, and the mountains which surround it on all sides are heavily timbered. It is a lovely place in summer, and the winters are not rigorous except upon the ranges; there the snows fall to great depths. But one of the principal attractions to the Indians was the large hot sulphur spring, to which they resorted for the cure of various ailments; a broad circular pool of hot steaming water, strongly impregnated with sulphur, soda and other minerals. It is fed by a constant flow from smaller springs in the neighboring hillside .... Trout swarmed in all the streams, and Grand lake, in which Grand River takes its rise, contains thousands of these beautiful fish. In the melting seasons Grand River runs full to the height of its banks. The Park being a sheltered retreat, well nigh inaccessible to their enemies, the plains Indians, and possessing all the advantages which an Indian desires, it is not surprising that the Utes should have made vigorous efforts to retain it.

1862 - Commissioner Dole: Colorado and WASH Gold Rushes Infringing on Indian Rights

Commissioner Dole, in 1862, confirmed that the Indians claimed the land:

> Considerable difficulty has been created in Colorado and Washington with the tribes in those Territories by the great increase of immigration, attracted by newly discovered gold mines. The Indians claim that the land belongs to them, while the miners, in search of new veins, are disposed to pay but little respect to their claims. A sufficient extent of country should be assigned to the Indians, and they should be protected in its enjoyment.[23]

March 1863 - Delegation of Cheyenne, Arapaho, Comanche, Kiowa and Caddo Chiefs Visit Washington, DC - Dissuade Them from Joining Confederacy

According to newspaper accounts:

> "The savages were dressed in full feather—buffalo robes, Indian tanned, and bead worked leggings, with a profusion of paints upon their faces and hair, etc. ... They squatted themselves down upon the floor in a semicircle—fourteen chiefs and two squaws—and were instantly surrounded by the curious crowd." One of the delegates, a Kiowa chief named Yellow Wolf, drew special attention for the large silver peace medal he wore, given to the Kiowas by President Thomas Jefferson. The medal had been handed down for generations and was held in the highest esteem by the tribe.

Two Cheyenne chiefs, Lean Bear and Spotted Wolf, each addressed the President, amazed at what they had seen. They pledged their tribal friendship but expressed dire concern about the encroachment of white settlers on their lands.

President Lincoln responded by telling the Indians that:

> "It is the object of this Government to be on terms of peace with you and all our red brethren. We constantly endeavor to be so. We make

treaties with you, and will try to observe them" Lincoln continued, "The palefaced people are numerous and prosperous because they cultivate the earth, produce bread, and depend upon the products of the earth rather than wild game for a subsistence. This is the chief reason of the difference; but there is another. Although we are now engaged in a great war between one another, we are not, as a race, so much disposed to fight and kill one another as our red brethren."[24]

The President was speaking truthfully when he said the U.S. would try to observe the treaties made with the Indians.[25] If fact, it was rarely done. As the President was seeking to secure peaceful relations with the Indians and to dissuade them from joining forces with the Confederacy, it was untoward to speak of the comparison of the two races in regard to warfare. In July of the same year, the Battle of Gettysburg would be fought with more than 50,000 estimated casualties alone, the bloodiest single battle of the Civil War. Also, many times reservations set aside were barren, arid and without irrigation making farming impossible.

1863 - Commissioner Dole to Governor/Superintendent Evans - Get Cheyenne and Arapaho that Have Not Signed Treaty of Fort Wise to Do So

Commissioner Dole wanted Governor Evans to get all of the Cheyenne and Arapaho that had not signed the Treaty of Fort Wise to do so. On July 16, 1863, Commissioner Dole wrote to Governor/Superintendent Evans: "I hope you will find it possible to arrange with the Cheyennes and Arapahos that have not signed the Treaty to do so and put them together, or make some other arrangement that will be just to them, and satisfactory to the whites."[26] In short, Governor/Superintendent Evans's top priority from the Indian Office was to secure the rest of the Indian signatories.

Aug. 1863 - Governor/Superintendent Evans Council with Cheyenne and Arapaho Leaders, Big Timbers

Governor Evans scheduled an Aug. 27, 1863, council with Cheyenne and Arapaho leaders at Big Timbers to get them to sign the Fort Wise Treaty. After traveling there, he received news that the Cheyenne were unable to meet due to widespread sickness that was circulating among them. Even though the Cheyenne's encampment on Beaver Creek was only located approximately twenty-five miles from the Republican River Council site, Governor Evans did not elect to travel to the diphtheria and whooping cough infested camp. In numerous instances, epidemics of diphtheria and whooping cough were fatal diseases in Indian communities, with high mortality rates among children and the elderly.[27]

Oct. 1863 - Commissioner Dole Confirms Mineral Wealth of CO TER

On Oct. 31, 1863, Commissioner Dole, confirmed the mineral wealth of the CO TER in his Annual Report to the Secretary of the Interior, without referring to the destitution and desperation of the Cheyenne and Arapaho which might lead to war:

> **Colorado Territory**, resting upon the headwaters of the Platte and Arkansas rivers and the western slope of the Rocky mountains, **is rich in mineral wealth, containing gold, silver, copper,** iron, coal and salt, alabaster, limestone, and gypsum. None but gold mines have been worked to any extent; these are proving remunerative ... (Emphasis added).[28]

He stressed the importance of the Treaty negotiated with the Tabeguache band of Utahs extinguishing their title to white settlements in Colorado, and more importantly to valuable mining districts:

> It will be seen that by the treaty negotiated with the Tabequache band of Utahs, as above stated, the **Indian title is extinguished to one among [sic] the largest and most valuable tracts of land ever ceded to the United States. It includes nearly all the important settlements thus far** made in Colorado, and all the valuable mining districts discovered up to this time. (Emphasis added).[29]

Oct. 1863 - Treaty of Conejos Only with Tabeguache Utes - Cede Land East of Continental Divide and Middle Park

White immigrants occupying Ute lands during the Colorado Gold Rush of 1858-59 and after the passage of the Homestead Act in 1862, increased Ute hostilities against the trespassers.

Anticipating more treaty negotiations with the Utes, Lafayette Head, Agent at the Conejos Indian Agency in the San Luis Valley, brought a Ute delegation to Washington, DC., in Feb. 1863. Leaders from each of Colorado's Ute bands, including the Tabeguache leaders Shavano and Ouray, rode a train to DC and visited New York City. It was clear that the trip was intended to favorably influence the U.S. position in negotiations, demonstrating that the Utes didn't stand a chance against a U.S. war given the strength in numbers and technology that would be brought to bear by the U.S.

On Oct. 7, 1863, at the Tabeguache Agency in Conejos, Governor John Evans, ex-officio Superintendent of Indian Affairs for Colorado, Michael Steck, Simeon Whitely and Lafayette Head negotiated a treaty with the Tabeguache Band of Utes. The U.S. had hoped that more of Colorado's Ute bands would sign the treaty, but only the Tabeguache were willing to attend the negotiations in any significant number.

The Tabeguache Utes relinquished claims to all land in Colorado's Rocky Mountains east of the Continental Divide, along with Middle Park. In exchange, the Tabeguache Utes were confined to a region that stretched from the Uncompahgre Valley in the west to the Sawatch Range in the east, and from the Colorado River valley in the north to the Gunnison River valley in the south. The Utes would receive $10,000 worth of annuities—food and provisions—each year for ten years.

Since the other Ute Bands didn't agree to allow miners, soldiers, and homesteaders to trespass or build on their land, the Conejos Treaty's objective to prevent violence failed. In addition, as with most other Indian treaties, the U.S. failed to provide the promised annuities; in 1865, just one year after the Treaty was ratified, Governor Evans was already complaining about a delay in annuity shipments.[30]

Nov. 1863 - Letter from Governor Evans to Commissioner Dole regarding Indian State of War

Governor Evans wrote to Commissioner Dole in Nov. 1863, based on a rumor of a white settler, that the Comanches, Apaches, Kiowas, the northern band of Arapahoes, and all of the Cheyennes, with the Sioux, were forming an alliance to go to war in the spring. Mexicans, along with the Comanche and Apache Indians, promised to help.

Executive Department, Denver, November 10, 1863.
Honorable W. P. Dole, Commissioner Indian Affairs: Statement of White Settler.

> Having recovered an Arapaho prisoner, a squaw, from the Utes, I obtained the confidence of the Indians completely. I have lived with them (Utes) from a boy, and my wife is an Arapaho. In honor of my exploit in recovering the prisoner the Indians recently gave me a "big medicine dance" about 55 miles below Fort Lyon, on the Arkansas River, at which the leading chiefs and warriors of several of the tribes of the plains met. The Comanches, Apaches, Kiowas, the northern band of Arapahoes, and all of the Cheyennes, with the Sioux, have pledged one another to go to war with the whites as soon as they can procure ammunition in the spring. ... There are a great many Mexicans with the Comanche and Apache Indians, all of whom urge on the war, promising to help the Indians themselves, and that a great many more Mexicans would come up from New Mexico for the purpose in the spring. John Evans, Governor Colorado Territory and ex officio Superintendent Indian Affairs.

MEMORANDA.

> I received letters from Major S. G. Colley, U.S. Indian agent for the Upper Arkansas, and from Major Loree, U.S. Indian agent for the Upper Platte Agency, as well as other corroboration of these statements, which were also sent forward with them. John Evans, Governor of Colorado Territory.[31]

April - May 1864 - Colorado Volunteer Forces Make Unprovoked Attacks on Cheyenne Villages in CO TER

Tensions between Colorado's burgeoning white population and the Cheyenne Indians reached a feverish pitch in the Spring of 1864. Colorado Volunteer forces made unprovoked attacks on Cheyenne villages in CO

TER. The Cheyenne retaliated by raiding mail and freight wagon trains, stage stations and outlying farms. Thus begin a period of conflict known as the Indian War of 1864.[32]

In skirmishes the 1st Regiment Colorado Volunteer Calvary announced that this one was the beginning of the war, creating a frenzy of excitement. The Rocky Mountain News printed a front-page editorial advocating the "extermination of the red devils" and urging its readers to "take a few months off and dedicate that time to wiping out the Indians."[33]

April 12, 1864 - Battle of Fremont's Orchard, Colorado Volunteer Cavalry and Cheyenne, NE/CO

The U.S. War Records document the Battle of Fremont's Orchard in April 1864.

Lieutenant Dunn of the 1st Regiment Colorado Volunteer Calvary encountered a group of Cheyenne, who had reportedly stolen livestock and downed telegraph lines in northeast Colorado. Although the initial contact with the Cheyenne was friendly, hostilities broke out when Lieutenant Dunn and his men attempted to disarm the group. The resulting fight became known as the Battle of Fremont's Orchard.

George L. Sanborn, Captain, First Colorado Cavalry, Commanding, requested 8,000 more cartridges for the carbines for his command.[34]

May 3, 1864 - Without Provocation, Colorado Volunteer Cavalry Attacks Peaceful Cheyenne Leaders at Cedar Bluffs, Kansas

Under the command of Lieutenant George S. Eayre, the 1st Regiment Colorado Volunteer Cavalry, part of Chivington's command, scouting for presumed "hostiles", carried out an attack on a camp of "friendly" Cheyennes under the leadership of Black Kettle and Lean Bear. When the soldiers were seen advancing in formation as if to attack, Lean Bear went out to meet them peacefully, with a number of Indians following him. He wore the medallion presented to him in Washington and carried official papers underlining his friendliness to the United States. As the small group neared the soldiers, Lieutenant Eayre gave the order to fire. Lean Bear and another leader, Star, fell to the ground. The soldiers then rode over to them and shot them again to make sure that they were dead. The attack at Cedar Bluffs was one of three fights that Chivington's troops had with Cheyennes in a little over a month's time and inaugurated a pattern of U.S. Army murders of Indian peace leaders.[35]

Major Downing's (First Colorado Cavalry) report did not mention Lean Bear. He stated:

> I then directed the men to confine their efforts to killing as many Indians as possible, which, after a fight of about three hours, they succeeded in killing about 25 Indians and wounding about 30 or 40 more, when the carbine ammunition getting rather scarce, and the Indians so concealed that after 50 shots I could scarcely get a men ... ***I believe now it is but the commencement of war with this treble [sic], which must result in exterminating them.*** (Emphasis added).[36]

May 31, 1864 - Letter to Major Wynkoop from Colonel Chivington, 'Whip Cheyennes'

Colonel Chivington directed Major E.W. Wynkoop as follows:

> "[T]he Cheyennes will have to be roundly whipped—or completely wiped out—before they will be quiet. I say that if any of them are caught in your vicinity, the only thing to do is kill them." He copied Captain William H. Backus on this order.[37]

Colonel Chivington's public speeches advocated killing all of the Indians in Colorado. A month later, while addressing a gathering of church deacons, he dismissed the possibility of making a treaty with the Cheyenne: "It simply is not possible for Indians to obey or even understand any treaty. I am fully satisfied, gentlemen, that to kill them is the only way we will ever have peace and quiet in Colorado."[38]

June 1, 1864 - Mystery of Hungate Family

On June 1, 1864, the Hungate Family was found murdered 25 miles southeast of Denver. Their mutilated bodies were brought to Denver and displayed, causing wide-spread panic. The coroner's inquest indicated the family "came to their death by being feloniously killed by some person or persons...supposed to be Indians."[39] The Hungate Massacre of 1864 crystallized public sentiment against the Indians, even though it was not confirmed that they were responsible for the killings.

1864 - Four Colorado Forts

In the summer of 1864, General Robert B. Mitchell received 1,000 troops to both patrol the Platte River Road and to establish outposts. At the same time, four sites were located and forts built throughout northeastern Colorado.[40]

Camp Rankin, renamed Fort Sedgwick, along the South Platte River near Julesburg and the stage route to Denver was assigned the responsibility of protecting wagon trains, pioneers, and the Overland Stage from Plains Indians in the area. The Iowa Volunteer Cavalry patrolled the Trail east and the Colorado Militia patrolled the area west of Julesburg. It is important to emphasize the use of volunteer militia in Colorado.

Further upstream, the South Platte Valley Station, near present day Sterling, was taken over for military use. This Station was built in 1859 and served from the beginning of the South Platte Trail to the end under four stage companies: The L&PP, the COC&PP, the Overland Stage Company, and Wells Fargo and Company.

Near the mouth of Bijou Creek, Camp Tyler was established. The construction of the post began by Colorado Volunteers under the leadership of General Sam Brown. It was soon renamed Camp Wardell as construction continued by "Galvanized Yankees" under the command of Captain Williams. These troops were Confederate soldiers released from prison because they joined the Union Army and moved west to fight the Indians. When the fort buildings were complete, a detachment of federal soldiers from the Missouri Cavalry under Lieutenant Colonel Willard Smith were garrisoned at the post, which was finally christened "Fort Morgan" in honor of Colonel Christopher A. Morgan. The post was about the size of one square city block.

In early 1864, Lieutenant Colonel William L. Collins, the commander of the Military Department of the Platte River, headquartered at Fort Laramie, Wyoming, came to the Cache la Poudre Valley in search of a location for a military post. To protect the Overland mail route that had recently been located through the region, Camp Collins was established on the Cache la Poudre River, near the settlement of Laporte. However, the post was short-lived, as a flood destroyed the camp in June 1864. Soon, the post was moved several miles further down the Cache la Poudre River, to present-day Fort Collins. Two 11th Ohio Volunteer Cavalry companies initially manned the post. The six square mile military reservation was renamed Fort Collins the following year. Soon, the town of Fort Collins grew up around the post.[41] Instead of using typical wooden stockades, these "citadels" were constructed of sod and adobe. By 1865, the Army had its forts established.[42]

June 3, 11, 13, 1864: Governor Evans Demands Federal Troops Be Sent to Denver

Governor Evans contacted Colonel Chivington, Major-General Curtis, General Carleton (NM) and General Mitchell to dispatch troops to Denver. Due to the ongoing Civil War and their commitment to other locales, they could not commit their troops. This meant that Colorado would have to use undertrained and undisciplined volunteer soldiers to "***whip these red-skin rebels into submission at once***" as directed by Governor Evans. (Emphasis added).

Letter from Governor Evans to Major-General Curtis, Commanding Department of Kansas, June 3, 1864

> It will be destruction and death to Colorado if our lines of communication are cut off, or if they are not kept so securely guarded as that freighters will not be afraid to cross the plains, especially by the Platte River, by which our subsistence comes. We are now short of provisions and but few trains are on the way. I would respectfully ask that our troops may be allowed to defend us and whip these red-skin rebels into submission at once. John Evans.[43]

Having received a letter reporting that the Indians had driven off stock from Mr. Van Wormer's ranch, burned his house, and murdered a man who was in Mr. Van Wormer's employ, his wife, and two children, and burned his house, Governor Evans, without confirming the veracity, ordered Colonel J. M. Chivington to "send a detachment of soldiers after [them] to recover the stock and chastise the Indians. As the Indians are probably a war party in considerable force, I suggest that the detachment be as strong as you can make it."[44]

In a letter from J. S. Maynard, Acting Assistant Adjutant-General, June 13, 1864, to Major C. S. Charlot, Assistant Adjutant General, Department of Kansas, Maynard expressed his concerns with the 1st Regiment Colorado Volunteer Calvary as never drilled and inefficient:

> [On the] afternoon of 11th, Indians stole 100 horses and mules from parties on Box Elder, Kiowa, and Coal Creeks, about 20 miles from Denver; burned houses on two ranches; murdered ranchman, his wife, two children; ravished woman before killing. I sent orders to Captain Davidson, commanding Company C (detained on Cherry Creek by flood), to send out a detachment of 50 men in pursuit, with orders to rejoin command en route to Lyon within two days; also ordered Lieutenant Chase, with detachment from Fremont's Orchard, in pursuit. ***Governor Evans has called upon militia, who are unmounted, never drilled, scattered, and consequently inefficient.*** Settlements so scattered they cannot be guarded. J. S. Maynard, Acting Assistant Adjutant-General. (Emphasis added).[45]

June 14, 1864: Governor Evans Wires Secretary of War to Muster Colorado Volunteer Cavalry into U.S. Service

When Governor Evans' demands for federal troops to be dispatched to Denver failed, he appealed directly to Secretary of War Edwin M. Stanton by wire on June 14, 1864, stating that Indians of the Colorado plains had committed "extensive murders" within a day's ride of Denver. He stated he could "furnish 100-days' men, if authorized to do so to fight Indians. Militia cannot be made useful, unless in the U.S. service, to co-operate with troops. Shall I call regiment of 100-days' men or muster into U.S. service the militia?"[46]

June 15, 1864: Major McKenny Warns General Curtis that Colorado's Volunteer Cavalry May Start Plains Indian War

Major T.I. McKenny who was sent to Fort Larned by General Curtis to assess the growing Indian hostilities in western Kansas reported:

> In regard to these Indian difficulties, I think if great caution is not exercised on our part there will be a bloody war. It should be our policy to try and conciliate them, guard our mails and trains well to prevent theft, and stop these (military) scouting **parties that are roaming over the country who do not know one tribe from the other, and who will kill anything in the shape of an Indian**. It will require but few murders on the part of our troops to unite all these warlike tribes of the plains who have been at peace for years and intermarried amongst one another. (Emphasis added).[47]

A day later, Governor Evans wrote to Major-General Curtis to whip the "infernal barbarians:"

> The Indian alliance is so strong that I am sure our settlement or our lines of communication cannot be protected without more force. I have applied for authority to raise a regiment of 100-days' men. I have also asked General Carleton to aid on the Arkansas and below. It is very important that Colonel Chivington operate with his command on these infernal Indians, and the troops under General Mitchell at Laramie, Cottonwood, and Kearny ought to be brought into service.

> I have ordered camps for friendly Indians at Fort Lyon, Fort Larned, and on the Cache la Poudre, and hope all the friendly bands of the Sioux may come to Fort Laramie; then, as we whip and destroy, others will join them, and we will bring it to a close. This requires vigorous war, and it can be effected soon. As we are at home powerless but to defend, and almost so even for that purpose, we rely upon you to pour down this hostile alliance of the infernal barbarians. I appeal to you to consider our situation, and to protect our lines of communication and our settlements by whipping these Indians. John Evans. (June 16, 1864).[48]

June 27, 1864: First Proclamation, Governor Evans, Colorado Superintendency Indian Affairs, Denver

Without any direction from the President or anyone else, Governor Evans issued a Proclamation to the Indians that the "Great Father is angry and will hunt them out and punish them." He ordered them to go to camps for friendly Indians at Fort Lyon, Fort Larned, and on the Cache la Poudre, and for the Sioux - Fort Laramie.

TO THE FRIENDLY INDIANS OF THE PLAINS:

Agents, interpreters, and traders will inform the friendly Indians of the plains that some members of their tribes have gone to war with the white people. They steal stock and run it off, hoping to escape detection and punishment. In some instances they have attacked and killed soldiers and murdered peaceable citizens. For this the Great Father is angry, and will certainly hunt them out and punish them, but he does not want to injure those who remain friendly to the whites. He desires to protect and take care of them. For this purpose I direct that all friendly Indians keep away from those who are at war, and go to places of safety. Friendly Arapahoes and Cheyennes belonging on the Arkansas River will go to Major Colley, U.S. Indian agent at Fort Lyon, who will give them provisions, and show them a place of safety. Friendly Kiowas and Comanches will go to Fort Larned, where they will be cared for in the same way. Friendly Sioux will go to their agent at Fort Laramie for directions. Friendly Arapahoes and Cheyennes of the Upper Platte will go to Camp Collins on the Cache la Poudre, where they will be assigned a place of safety and provisions will be given them.

The object of this is to prevent friendly Indians from being killed through mistake. None but those who intend to be friendly with the whites must come to these places. The families of those who have gone to war with the whites must be kept away from among the friendly Indians. The war on hostile Indians will be continued until they are all effectually subdued.[49]

Given his belligerent language about the President's "anger" and how the

President intends to hunt them down and punish them, it was unlikely that any Indian would go to a military fort. Governor Evans continued to exhort war on "hostile Indians," without any authority.

August 10, 1864: Governor Evans Requests 10,000 U.S. Troops from Secretary of War; Requests Commissioner Dole to Lobby for His Troops Request

Governor Evans vituperative language accelerated on a daily basis. On August 10, 1864, he wrote to Secretary of War Stanton that Denver was on the verge of destruction from the "largest Indian war" of all the Plains Indians.

Denver, Colorado, August 10, 1864, Honorable E. M. Stanton:

> The alliance of Indians on the plains reported last winter in my communication is now undoubted. A large force, say 10,000 troops, will be necessary to defend the lines and put down hostilities. Unless they can be sent at once we will be cut off and destroyed. John Evans, Governor of Colorado Territory.[50]

Denver City, Colorado, August 10, 1864. Honorable W. P. Dole, Commissioner of Indian Affairs:

> I am now satisfied that the tribes of the plains are nearly all combined in this terrible war, as apprehended last winter. It will be the largest Indian war this country ever had, extending from Texas to the British lines, involving nearly all the wild tribes of the plains. Please bring all the force of your department to bear in favor of speedy re-enforcements of our troops, and get me authority to raise a regiment of 100-days' mounted men. Our militia law is inoperative, and unless this authority is given we will be destroyed. John Evans, Governor of Colorado Territory and Superintendent of Indians.[51]

August 11, 1864: Governor Evans Proclamation to Citizens of Colorado Authorizing Them to Kill Hostile Indians

The next day, Governor Evans issued a Proclamation to the citizenry of

Colorado that the Indians had refused to come into the forts he designated for their safety. He explicitly authorized settlers to organize killing parties targeting Indians perceived as a threat; to take captives; and to hold "for their private use and benefit" any property they capture. Evans further offered to furnish arms and ammunition and to pay any parties that will organize under the militia law of the territory to seek out and kill Indians, recruiting citizens to join the hundred-day volunteers for which Evans had been lobbying Secretary of War Stanton. He had no authority at this time to basically declare war.

PROCLAMATION.

Having sent special messengers to the Indians of the plains, directing the friendly to rendezvous at Fort Lyon, Fort Larned, Fort Laramie, and Camp Collins for safety and protection, warning them that all hostile Indians would be pursued and destroyed, and the last of said messengers having now returned, and the evidence being conclusive that most of the Indian tribes of the plains are at war and hostile to the whites, and having to the utmost of my ability endeavored to induce all of the Indians of the plains to come to said places of rendezvous, promising them subsistence and protection, which, with a few exceptions, they have refused to do:

Now, therefore, I, John Evans, governor of Colorado Territory, do issue this my proclamation, authorizing all citizens of Colorado, either individually or in such parties as they may organize, to go in pursuit of all hostile Indians on the plains, scrupulously avoiding those who have responded to my said call to rendezvous at the points indicated; also, to kill and destroy, as enemies of the country, wherever they may be found, all such hostile Indians. And further, as the only reward I am authorized to offer for such services, I hereby empower such citizens, or parties of citizens, to take captive, and hold to their own private use and benefit, all the property of said hostile Indians that they may capture, and to receive for all stolen property recovered from said Indians such reward as may be deemed proper and just therefor.

I further offer to all such parties as will organize under the militia law of the Territory for the purpose to furnish them arms and ammunition, and to present their accounts for pay as regular soldiers for themselves, their horses, their subsistence, and transportation, to Congress, under the assurance of the department commander that they will be paid.

The conflict is upon us, and all good citizens are called upon to do their duty for the defense of their homes and families.

In testimony whereof, I have hereunto set my hand and caused the great seal of the Territory of Colorado to be affixed this 11th day of August, A. D. 1864. John Evans.[52]

Analysis of Governor Evans' Second Proclamation of August 11, 1864 - University of Denver's John Evans Study Committee

The Report of the University of Denver's John Evans Study Committee, of November 2014, castigated Governor Evans.

> Evans's Proclamation of August 11 essentially created an unregulated vigilante force. ... No criteria are offered for violence-hungry settlers, who have been bombarded with anti-Indian sentiment from the state, the military, and local newspapers, and who would be outfitted and paid by the state, to differentiate hostile from friendly Indians. The proclamation does not merely carry a "vigilante tone," ... it is a blanket endorsement of citizen violence against Native people in partnership with territorial civil leadership.
>
> The policy laid out in this fateful document was tantamount to a declaration of war, and it was one which Evans had no legal authority to make.
>
> As for issuing such a proclamation as Superintendent of Indian Affairs, not in any stretch of the imagination could the laws that were in place at the time be interpreted as permitting a superintendent to send cadres of armed citizens to exterminate and loot unidentified Indian people.

In the direct aftermath of these events Colonel John Chivington declared martial law on August 23, 1864, at the request of Denver businessmen who "hoped to promote enlistments of 100-day men to rid our territory of all hostile Indians."

According to Gary Roberts, Evans chillingly "told Wynkoop matters were out of his hand, and that the Indians needed to be punished more to insure peace. More than once Evans asked, 'What will I do with the 3rd Regiment if I make peace?' He told Wynkoop, 'The 3rd Regiment was raised to kill Indians, and kill Indians it must.'" Evans asserted that his credibility in Washington would be lost if, having agitated so stridently for war, he now made peace.[53]

August 12, 1864: 3rd Regiment Authorized for 100 Days

On August 12, 1864, Evans finally received his authorization for the 3rd Regiment, but the term of enlistment was only for 100 days, prompting the Rocky Mountain News to hail the 3rd as the "Hundredazers."

On August 13, 1864, C. S. Charlot, Assistant Adjutant-General, authorized the regiment.

> *Colonel John M. Chivington, Denver*
>
> *Your Governor has been authorized to raise a mounted 100-days' regiment. The ordnance, quartermaster, and commissary officers in your district will furnish the necessary supplies upon proper requisitions.* (Emphasis added).[54]

August 18, 1864: Governor Evans Sends Letter to Secretary of War that Colorado Is in Danger of Destruction from Indians

On August 18, 1864, Governor Evans raised the stakes in a letter to Secretary of War Stanton:

> Extensive Indian depredations, with murder of families, occurred yesterday thirty miles south of Denver. Our lines of communication are cut, and our crops, our sole dependence, are all in exposed

localities, and cannot be gathered by our scattered population. ***Large bodies of Indians are undoubtedly near to Denver, and we are in danger of destruction both from attacks of Indians and starvation.*** I earnestly request that Colonel Ford's regiment, Second Colorado Volunteers, be immediately sent to our relief. It is impossible to exaggerate our danger. We are doing all we can for our defense. Jno. Evans, Governor. (Emphasis added).[55]

August 19, 1864: Secretary of War Informs Governor Evans, due to Civil War There Is Shortage of U.S. Army Troops

Even though there was a shortage of soldiers due to the Civil War, on August 19, 1864, Secretary Stanton ordered troops to Colorado.

> Orders have been sent General Rosecrans to send the Colorado regiment of cavalry to your Territory if he can possibly spare it. Edwin M. Stanton, Secretary of War.[56]

August 29, 1864: Chief Black Kettle and Other Chiefs Have Letters Sent to Agent Colley and Major Wynkoop Seeking Peace Talks

George Bent, son of trader William Bent and his Cheyenne wife Owl Woman, and Edmund Guerrier, another mixed blood, wrote letters to Indian Agent S.G. Colley and the commander of Fort Lyon, Major Wynkoop, on behalf of Chief Black Kettle and other chiefs, seeking peace talks in response to Governor Evans Proclamation. As noted below, repeated efforts for peace were sought by the Cheyenne and Arapaho for naught. Governor Evans was bent on war.

Sep. 4-18, 1864: Chief Black Kettle Letter, Peace Talk Request Delivered to Major Wynkoop; Major Wynkoop Meets with Black Kettle at Smoky Hill River and Confirms Cheyenne and Arapaho Seeking Peace; Wynkoop Agrees to Escort Cheyenne and Arapaho Chiefs to Meet with Governor Evans regarding Peace

Sep. 4: Cheyenne Chief One Eye, his wife, and a Cheyenne named Min-im-mic deliver the Bent/Guerrier letter to Fort Lyon. Major Wynkoop sees this as an opportunity to restore peace and free several white hostages, who the chiefs have offered in exchange for Cheyenne prisoners.

Sep. 6-18: Major Wynkoop rides out from Fort Lyon with 127 men to meet with Chief Black Kettle and other leaders on the Smoky Hill River. During the meeting, the Cheyenne and Arapaho Chiefs agree to turn over 4 white children taken as captives. Wynkoop agrees to escort Chief Black Kettle and other Cheyenne and Arapaho chiefs to meet with Governor John Evans.[57]

Sep. 4, 1864: Governor Evans Informed by Indian Agent Colley that Cheyenne and Arapaho Desire Peace

On Sep. 4, 1864, Governor Evans, Superintendent of Indian Affairs, was informed in writing of the Cheyenne and Arapaho's plea for peace:

> Two Cheyenne Indians and one squaw have just arrived at this post. They report that nearly al (sic) of the Arapahoes, most of the Cheyennes, and two large bands of Ogallala and Brule Sioux are encamped near the "Bunch of Timbers" some 80 to 100 miles northeast of this place; that they have sent runners to the Comanches, Apaches, Kiowas, and Sioux requesting them to make peace with the whites. They brought a letter purporting to be signed by Black Kettle and other chiefs, a copy * [Not Found] of which is here enclosed. They say that the letter was written by George Bent, a half-breed son of W.W. Bent, late U.S. Indian agent for this agency. They also state that the Indians have seven prisoners. One says four women and three children, the other states three women and four children. Major Wynkoop has put these Indians in the guard- house, and requested that they be well treated in order that he may be able to rescue the white prisoners from the Indians. S. G. Colley, U.S. Indian Agent, Upper Arkansas.[58]

Sep. 14, 1864: Governor Evans Forwards Agent Colley's Letter that Cheyenne and Arapaho Desire Peace to Colonel Chivington

Sep. 14, 1864, Colonel J. M. Chivington, Commanding District of Colorado:

I herewith enclose for your information a copy of a letter received from Major Colley, U.S. Indian agent, Upper Arkansas Agency, dated September

4, 1864, Fort Lyon, stating the location of the Arapahoes and portions of other tribes of Indians, and inclosing a proposition for peace from Black Kettle and other chiefs. Jno. Evans, Governor of Colorado Territory.[59]

Sep. 18, 1864: Major Wynkoop Reports Meeting with Cheyenne and Arapaho regarding Peace to Acting Assistant Adjutant-General, District of Upper Arkansas

Fort Lyon, Colorado Territory, September 18, 1864.
Lieutenant J. E. Tappan, Acting Assistant Adjutant-General, District of Upper Arkansas:

> ***They came, as they stated, bearing with them a proposition for peace from Black Kettle and other chiefs of the Cheyenne and Arapahoe Nations.*** Their propositions were to the effect that they, the Cheyennes and Arapahoes, had in their possession seven white prisoners whom they offered to deliver up in case that we should come to terms of peace with them. They told me that the Cheyennes, Arapahoes, and Sioux were congregated for mutual protection, at what is called "Bunch of Timber," on headwaters of the Smoky Hill, at a distance of 140 miles northeast of this post numbering altogether about 3,000 warriors, and desirous to make peace with the whites. I told them I was not authorized to conclude terms of peace with them, but if they acceded to my proposition I would take what chiefs they might choose to select to the Governor of Colorado Territory and state the circumstances to him, and that I believed it would result in what it was their desire to accomplish, viz, peace with their white brethren. I had reference particularly to the Cheyenne and Arapahoe tribes ... they brought and turned over into my possession four white prisoners, all that was possible at the time being for them to turn over, the balance of the seven being, as they stated, with another band far to the northward ... I have the principal chiefs of the two tribes with me, and propose starting immediately to Denver City, Colorado Territory, to put into effect the proposition made aforementioned by me to them. E. W. Wynkoop, Major First Cavalry of Colorado, Commanding Post. (Emphasis added).[60]

Sep. 28, 1864: Governor Evans Meets with Cheyenne and Arapaho Peace Party; Rejects Peace Offer Alleging State of War with Military in Control

Sep. 1864 The Cheyenne and Arapaho seeking peace, traveled to Denver for a meeting with Governor and Superintendent of Indian Affairs Evans seeking peace. Governor Evans and Colonel Chivington met with the Cheyenne and Arapaho Chiefs at Camp Weld, near Denver.

Sep. 28, 1864 Meeting at Camp Weld

> We have come with our eyes shut, following [Major Wynkoop's] handful of men like coming through the fire. All we ask is that we have peace with the whites. We want to hold you by the hand. You are our father. We have been traveling thro' a cloud. The sky has been dark ever since the war began. These braves who are with me are all willing to do what I say. We want to take good tidings home to our people, that they may sleep in peace. I want you to give all the chiefs of these soldiers to understand that we are for peace, and that we have made peace, that we may not be mistaken by them for enemies. I have not come here with a little wolf bark, but have come to talk plain with you. We must live near the buffalo or starve. When we came here we came free, without any apprehension to see you, and when I go home and tell my people that I have taken your hand, and the hand of all the chiefs here in Denver, they will feel well, and so will all the different tribes of Indians on the Plains, after we have eaten and drank with them.[61]

Evans accused the leaders—men who had already signed the Fort Wise Treaty and who had now come to him at great personal risk—of being allied with the Lakota and having committed depredations …

Several of the Indians in attendance responded, asserting, "This is a mistake. We have made no alliance with the Sioux, or anyone else."

As the meeting report shows, the Cheyenne and Arapaho also pointed out that they did not know the reasons for the fighting launched by Chivington's forces in the three battles of the spring, with White Antelope raising this question to Evans, who simply ignored it.

Toward the end of the meeting, Evans claimed that he was obligated to turn the Cheyenne and Arapaho over to the Army, given his claim that the settlers and Indian peoples were at war: ***"Another reason that I am not in a condition to make a treaty, is that war is begun, and the power to make a treaty of peace has passed from me to the Great War Chief,"*** he asserted. (Emphasis added).[62]

> When faced with a last desperate attempt by leaders from those nations to make a peace that might have changed the trajectory of events, Evans blamed and rebuffed them, and arbitrarily, without sufficient cause, passed off his authority to the military. This pattern of irresponsible leadership amounted to dereliction of his duties as superintendent.
>
> This statement is particularly startling as it clearly indicates an abdication of his responsibility under Commissioner Dole's instruction, as well as in his role of Indian Superintendent, to negotiate for peace at every opportunity.[63]

Sep. 29, 1864: Governor Evans Sends False Letter to Major Curtis, U.S. Army, that Sioux Plan to Attack Colorado

Denver, September 29, 1864. Major-General Curtis:

> A party of the most reliable chiefs of Cheyennes and Arapahoe tribes, brought in by Major Wynkoop, say a very large party of Minneconjou and other Sioux Indians from the north are now on the Republican, nearly opposite the Cottonwood; that they soon will strike the Platte and make for the settlements of Colorado. General Sully has doubtless driven them down upon us. We must have a strong force after them at once or we will be destroyed by their cutting off our communication. Jno. Evans, Governor. Colorado Superintendency of Indian Affairs.[64]

Sep. 29, 1864: Governor Evans Sends Letter to Agent Colley regarding Meeting with Cheyenne and Arapaho Peace Party; That He Rejected Peace Offer due to U.S. State of War

Denver, September 29, 1864. S. G. Colley, U.S. Indian Agent:

> The chiefs brought in by Major Wynkoop have been heard. I have declined to make any treaty with them, lest it might embarrass the military operations against the hostile Indians of the plains. ***The Arapahoe and Cheyenne Indians being now at war with the United States Government must make peace with the military authorities.*** Of course this arrangement relieves the Indian Bureau of their care until peace is declared with them, and as their tribes are yet scattered, and all except Friday's band are at war, it is not probable that it will be done immediately. You will be particular to impress upon these chiefs the fact that my talk with them was for the purpose of ascertaining their views and not to offer them anything whatever. They must deal with the military authorities until peace, in which case alone they will be in proper position to treat with the Government in relation to the future. Jno. Evans, Governor Colorado Territory and ex- officio Supt. of Indian Affairs. (Emphasis added).[65]

Sep. 29, 1864: Governor Evans Forwards Letter from Agent Colley to Colonel Chivington that Cheyenne and Arapaho Peace Offer Denied

Fort Leavenworth, September 29, 1864. To John Evans:

> General Mitchell is hunting Indians up the Platte, and General Blunt south of Arkansas also searching for them. Try and give them any information you think reliable. The chiefs you named are not reliable, and desire to save their friends, who are near the Arkansas, by extravagant reports of forces elsewhere. They ought to be made to go and show our enemies. Their chiefs are all implicated in the attacks where they have depredated. All they fear is winter approaching and therefore they desire peace, which they cannot have at present. I was far up the Republican and Mitchell was farther. I will try to have new scouts sent out from Cottonwood to ascertain the truth of this report. If such a force is there it must be attacked as soon as possible. ***The idea of Sioux being driven down by Sully is not reasonable***; that was the report before my visit to the Platte, and I found nothing to justify it. S. R. Curtis, Major-General. (Emphasis added).[66]

October 14, 1864: Colonel Chivington Orders Captain Nichols, Colorado Third Regiment, to Kill All Indians He Encounters

Headquarters District of Colorado, Denver, October 14, 1864.
Captain D. H. Nichols, Third Regiment Colorado Cav., Valley Station, Colorado Territory:

> Captain: Be vigilant. ***Kill all the Indians you come across.*** Strengthen your squads at stations below you to Julesburg. Ammunition leaves by tomorrow's coach.
> J. M. Chivington, Colonel, Commanding District. (Emphasis added).[67]

October 15, 1864: Commissioner Dole Orders Governor Evans to Negotiate for Peace with Indians when They Offer, Regardless of U.S. State of War

> Sir: I have the honor to acknowledge the receipt of your letter of the 29th ultimo, stating that at a council held with certain Arapahoes and Cheyenne Indians, you informed them, in answer to their expressed desire for peace, that you had no treaty to make with them, that they must make terms with the military authority. In reply, I have to say that while I approve of your course as a matter of necessity, while these Indians and the military authorities are at war, and the civil authority is in abeyance, yet, as ***superintendent of Indian affairs, it is your duty to hold yourself in readiness to encourage and receive the first intimations of a desire on the part of the Indians for a permanent peace, and to cooperate with the military in securing a treaty of peace and amity.***
>
> I cannot help believing that very much of the difficulty on the plains might have been avoided, if a spirit of conciliation had been exercised by the military and others. (Emphasis added).[68]

November 4, 1864: Major Wynkoop Relieved of Command

Orders relieving Major Wynkoop of command and directing him to report to district headquarters at Fort Riley in Kansas are issued.

I. Major E. W. Wynkoop, First Cavalry of Colorado, is hereby relieved from the command of Fort Lyon, Colorado Territory, and is ordered to report without delay to headquarters District of the Upper Arkansas, for orders. II. Major Scott J. Anthony, First Cavalry of Colorado, will proceed to Fort Lyon, Colorado Territory, and assume command of that post, and report in regard to matters as stated in Special Orders, No. 4, paragraph VII, from these headquarters, dated Fort Riley, October 17, 1864. By order of Major Henning: A. Helliwell, Lieutenant and Acting Assistant Adjutant-General.[69]

November 15, 1864: Majors Anthony and Wynkoop Meet with Cheyenne and Arapaho Who Continue to Press for Peace

Major Anthony (New Commander at Fort Lyon) and Major Wynkoop (Relieved of Fort Lyon Command) met with about 60 Cheyenne and Arapaho chiefs and headmen at Fort Lyon.

Major Anthony advised the Cheyenne to return to their camps at Sand Creek and allowed the Arapaho under Little Raven to move down the Arkansas about 60 miles and there wait until he received further instructions from his superior officers. (Emphasis added).[70]

November 15, 1864: Commissioner Dole Reports to Secretary of Interior that Cheyenne and Arapaho Urge Peace - Military Says Further Punishment Needed

> ... on the 4th of September Agent Colley forwarded to the superintendent a letter signed by several of the Cheyenne chiefs, proposing terms of peace. On the 28th an interview took place between Governor Evans and these chiefs, at which, it appears, from the annual report of that officer, they seemed earnest for peace; but the governor deemed it his duty, under the existing circumstances, to decline acceding to their terms, or indeed to make any terms with them, and the interview ended with leaving the chiefs referred to, or any others who might be disposed towards peace, to communicate with the military authorities. This course seems, from the paper accompanying Governor Evans's report, to have commended itself

to Major General Curtis as the proper one to be pursued, that ***officer deeming it necessary, in order to a permanent peace and the future good behavior of the Indians, that they should receive further punishment;*** ... ***Governor Evans advocates the policy of a winter expedition against the offending tribes.*** (Emphasis added).[71]

November 16, 1864: Major Anthony Reports to Headquarters that Cheyenne and Arapaho Appealing for Peace

Headquarters, Fort Lyon, Colorado Territory, November 16, 1864.

SIR: I have the honor to report that since my last report on the 7th [6th] instant the Cheyenne Indians, numbering about 200, under their head chief, Black Kettle, have sent into the post a request to meet me for a council. I met them and had a talk. They profess friendship for the whites, and say they never desired war, and do not now. They were very desirous of visiting the post and coming in with their whole band. I would not permit this, ***but told them they might camp on Sound [sic] [Sand] Creek, twenty-five miles northeast of the post, until the pleasure of the commanding officer of the district could be learned.*** They appear to want peace, and want someone authorized to make a permanent settlement of all troubles with them to meet them and agree upon terms. I told them that I was not authorized as yet to say that any permanent peace could be established, but that no war would be waged against them until your pleasure was heard. ***I am satisfied that all of the Arapahoes and Cheyennes who have visited this post desire peace*** ... Neither of these tribes are satisfied with me for not permitting them to visit the post, and cannot understand why I will not make peace with them. ***My intention, however, is to let matters remain dormant until troops can be sent out to take the field against all the tribes.*** Scott J. Anthony, Major First Cavalry of Colorado, Commanding Post. (Emphasis added).[72]

November 28, 1864: Major Anthony Reports Arrival of Colorado Third Regiment at Fort Lyon: 1000 Soldiers

Fort Lyon, Colorado Territory, November 28, 1864. Lieutenant A.

Helliwell, Acting Assistant Adjutant-General, Fort Riley, Kansas:

> SIR: I have the honor to report that Colonel John M. Chivington, First Cavalry of Colorado, arrived at this post this day with 1,000 men of the Third Regiment Colorado Cavalry (100-day's men) and two howitzers, on expedition against Indians. This number of men has been required for some time, and is appreciated by me now, as I believe *the Indians will be properly punished—what they have for some time deserved*. I go out with 125 men and two howitzers to join his command. Scott J. Anthony, Major First Cavalry of Colorado, Commanding Post. (Emphasis added).[73]

November 28, 1864: Major General Curtis Reports to Brigadier General Carleton that Cheyenne and Arapaho Are Begging for Peace

Headquarters Department of Kansas, Fort Leavenworth,
November 28, 1864. Brigadier General J. H. Carleton, Commanding Department of New Mexico:

> General: ... *The Arapahoes and Cheyennes have come into Lyon begging for peace*, turning over prisoners, horses, &c., for that purpose. The hardest kind of terms are demanded by me and conceded by some of these Indians. They insist on peace or absolute sacrifice, as I choose. Of course, they will have to be received, but *there still remains some of these tribes and all the Kiowas to attend to, and I have proposed a winter campaign for their benefit. This, if successful, must be secret* and well-arranged beforehand. I have written the War Department, and Governor Evans, of Colorado, has gone to Washington to urge my plans. S. R. Curtis, Major-General. (Emphasis added).[74]

November 29, 1864: Sand Creek Massacre - Colonel Chivington Reports Killing 400-500 Indians; Scalped Every Man, Woman and Child, Mutilated Their Bodies; Removed Private Parts as War Trophies

On November 29, 1864, from in the field at the South Bend of the Big Sandy, John M. Chivington, First Colorado Cavalry, reported:

In the last ten days my command has marched 300 miles, 100 of which the snow was two feet deep. After a march of forty miles last night I, at daylight this morning, attacked Cheyenne village of 130 lodges, from 900 to 1,000 warriors strong; **killed Chiefs Black Kettle, White Antelope, Knock Knee, and Little Robe [Little Raven], and between 400 and 500 other Indians**, and captured as many ponies and mules. Our loss, 9 killed, 38 wounded. All died nobly. ***Think I will catch some more of them eighty miles, on Smoky Hill.*** Found white man's scalp, not more than three days' old, in one of lodges. (Emphasis added).[75]

Report on Sand Creek Massacre by Indian Agent Leavenworth

I have the honor to enclose herewith papers relating to the late massacre of friendly Indians by Colonel J.M. Chivington,* near Fort Lyon. It is impossible for me to express to you the horror with which I view this transaction; it has destroyed the last vestige of confidence between the red and white man. ***Nearly every one of the chiefs and headmen of the Arapahoe and Cheyenne tribes who had remained true to the whites, and were determined not to fight the whites, were cruelly murdered*** when resting in all the confidence of assurances from Major Wynkoop, and I also believe from Major Anthony, that they should not be disturbed. Major Wynkoop, of the Colorado cavalry, was doing all that it was possible for an officer to do to pacify the Indians, and had restored comparative peace to this frontier, when all his work was destroyed, and an Indian war inaugurated that must cost the government millions of money and thousands of lives. These are the bitter fruits of Governor Evans's proclamation that I sent you last summer: "to the victor belongs the spoils." I then stated that those men could not stop to inquire if the Indians they should come in contact with were friendly or hostile. When Major Wynkoop went to Denver with the chiefs of tribes under his charge, why did Governor Evans refuse to act in any way, for or against them ... they were determined not to fight the whites... Little Bear escaped with his band; and it is due to him and to humanity that no effort be spared, in my opinion, to save him and his from certain destruction. I'm making every effort possible to find the Comanches and Kiowas; but I have little hope of succeeding. J. H. Leavenworth, U.S. Indian Agent (Emphasis added).

*The papers referred to above were not received.⁷⁶

Sand Creek Massacre Reported as "Disastrous and Shameful Occurrence"

Most disastrous and shameful occurrence of all, the massacre of a large number of men, women and children of the Indians of this agency by the troops under command of Colonel Chivington, of the United States volunteer cavalry of Colorado. ... Several hundred of them had come in to a place designated by Governor Evans as a rendezvous for those who would separate themselves from the hostile parties, these Indians were set upon and butchered in cold blood by troops in the service of the United States.⁷⁷

> The Sand Creek Indian Fight. - This memorable struggle for the permanent immunity of southern Colorado from strife with hostile Indians began on September 9th and ended on December 29, 1864, thus lasting one hundred and twelve days. Mr. Stubbs was an active participant in it from the beginning to the end, as a member of Company G, Third Colorado Cavalry. His company was formed at Denver and went into camp four miles below Pueblo, and a few days later marched down the Arkansas River to Fort Lyon, being three days on the march and suffering many hardships therein. The soldiers were obliged to sleep on the snow, and as the emergency was great, all men whom they met on the road were impressed into the service despite its hardships. At nine o'clock one night the force was ordered out to march north and surprise the enemy. After spending the whole night on the march, and being led by their scouts and half-breed Indian guides through a pond, in which the horses floundered and the men suffered intensely from the cold, the Cheyenne Indian village was discovered at a distance of three miles from the camp at sunrise on the morning of November 29th. The men then became wild with excitement and could not be restrained, but rushed upon the Indians, who were still sleeping and unprepared for the attack. The noise awakened them and numbers succeeded in escaping, but five hundred of the nine hundred in the band were killed, with the loss of only one man of Company G, whose fate was due to his own carelessness. The battle lasted until five o'clock in the evening

and during its progress two cannon were used by the whites to great advantage. Company G found a high enjoyment in burning the tepees of the Indians after the latter were routed. On the morning of November 30th they marched to the junction of Sand creek with the Arkansas and went into camp ... Nearby they found Indians in force and drove them far into the plains. On December 3d the company was ordered home. ... This war freed southern Colorado from the danger of savage attacks and established lasting security for the settlers. Mr. Stubbs escaped without injury.[78]

December 7, 1864: Colonel Chivington's Second Report to Governor Evans: Killed 500 Indians, Still in Pursuit of Cheyenne and Arapaho

December 7, 1864. Governor John Evans

Had fight with Cheyennes forty miles north of Lyon. I lost 9 killed and 38 wounded. **Killed 500 Indians**; destroyed 130 lodges; took 500 mules and ponies. Marched 300 miles in ten days; snow two feet deep for 100 miles. **Am still after them.** J. M. Chivington, Colonel, Commanding District of Colorado and First Indian Expedition. (Emphasis added).[79]

December 15, 1864: Major Anthony Reports Sand Creek Massacre Was Terrible but Should Be Done to All Hostile Tribes

Headquarters Fort Lyon, Colorado Territory, December 15, 1864.

> ... *The massacre was a terrible one and such a one as each of the hostile tribes on the plains richly deserve.* I think one such visitation to each hostile tribe would forever put an end to Indian war on the plains, and I regret exceedingly that this punishment could not have fallen upon some other band. Major Anthony, Major First Cavalry of Colorado, Commanding Post (Emphasis added).[80]

Governor Evans Culpability in Sand Creek Massacre - University of Denver's John Evans Study Committee

Evans abrogated his duties as superintendent, fanned the flames of war when he could have dampened them, cultivated an unusually interdependent relationship with the military, and rejected clear opportunities to engage in peaceful negotiations with the Indian peoples under his jurisdiction. Furthermore, he successfully lobbied the War Department for the deployment of a federalized regiment who executed the worst of the atrocities during the massacre.[81]

January 16, 1865: Sand Creek Military Investigation

Major General S. R. Curtis, Fort Leavenworth, Department of Kansas. Fort Lyon, Colorado Territory, January 16, 1865.

>Personally appeared before me Lieutenant James D. Cannon, First New Mexico Volunteer Infantry, who, after being duly sworn, says: That on the 28th day of November, 1864, I was ordered by Major Scott J. Anthony to accompany him on an Indian expedition as his battalion adjutant. The object of that expedition was to be a thorough campaign against hostile Indians, as I was led to understand. *I referred to the fact of there being a friendly camp of Indians in the immediate neighborhood, and remonstrated against simply attacking that camp, as I was aware that they were resting there in fancied security under promises held out to them of safety from Major E. W. Wynkoop, former commander of the post at Fort Lyon, as well as by Major S. J. Anthony, then in command.* Our battalion was attached to the command of Colonel J. M. Chivington, and left Fort Lyon on the night of the 28th of November, 1864. About daybreak on the morning of the 29th of November we came in sight of the camp of the friendly Indians aforementioned, and was ordered by Colonel Chivington to attack the same, which was accordingly done. The command of Colonel Chivington was composed of about 1,000 men. The village of the Indians consisted of from 100 to 130 lodges, and, as far as I am able to judge, of from 500 to 600 souls, the majority of which were women and children. In going over the battle-ground next day I did not see a body of man, woman, or child but was scalped, and in many instances their bodies were mutilated in the most horrible manner -- men, women, and children's privates cut out, &c. I heard one man say that he had cut a woman's private parts out, and had them for exhibition on a stick. I heard another

man say that he had cut the fingers off of an Indian to get the rings on the hand. According to the best of my knowledge and belief, these atrocities that were committed were with the knowledge of J. M. Chivington, and I do not know of him taking any measures to prevent them. I heard of one instance of a child a few months' old being thrown in the feed-box of a wagon, and after being carried some distance left on the ground to perish. I also heard of numberless instances in which men had cut out the private parts of females and stretched them over the saddle bows, and wore them over their hats while riding in the ranks. All these matters were a subject of general conversation, and could not help being known by Colonel J. M. Chivington. James D. Cannon, First Lieutenant, First Infantry, New Mexico Volunteers. Sworn and subscribed to before me this 27th day of January, 1865, at Fort Lyon, Colorado Territory W. P. Minton, Second Lieutenant, First New Mexico Volunteers, Post Adjutant. (Emphasis added).[82]

1865: U.S. Condemns Sand Creek Massacre

After a lengthy investigation of the Sand Creek Massacre, the U.S. condemned it and decided to offer reparations to the afflicted parties in exchange for peace. In addition, the removal of the Cheyenne and Arapaho from Colorado was part of the U.S.' renewed focus on pacifying the indigenous population of the American West to make way for homesteads, railroads, mines, and cities.

April 28, 1865: Treaty with Arapaho and Cheyenne for Colorado Land, Offer No Money, No Specific Land for New Reservation

By the Spring of 1865, President Abraham Lincoln appointed Vital Jarrot as the Indian Agent to the Upper Platte Agency. He had served in the leading role of Adjutant General during the Black Hawk War in 1832 in which Lincoln served as a volunteer.[83]

On April 28, 1865, Jarrot was notified by Charles Mix, Acting Commissioner, that President Lincoln had selected him to head the Upper Platte Agency based on his "influence ... arising from your long residence among and intimate acquaintance." He was to negotiate with the Arapaho,

Cheyenne and Sioux affiliated with them and Cheyenne for a cession of their lands. His instructions were as follows:

> Agreements to pay money will not be approved. If a treaty is made, it will be one of occupancy only: no title to lands will be acknowledged in the Indians of the country they abandon, nor will any be conferred upon them in the country they are to inhabit; Just an article may be inserted providing that the whites will be excluded from settlement in the country assigned to them.[84]

1865: Superintendent Taylor, Upper Platte; Obstruction of Mining Prejudicial to U.S.

Edward B. Taylor, Superintendent, Upper Platte, advised that obstruction to the development of the mines in this region should be avoided:

> *The precious metals, our sole reliance to liquidate the accruing interest upon the national debt*, are derived chiefly from the mining districts of Colorado, Oregon, California, Nevada, Idaho, and Montana, and any barrier which obstructs emigration to these mines, and retards their development, must prove highly prejudicial to the financial prosperity of the country. (Emphasis added).[85]

October 11-13, 1865: U.S. Treaty Delegation, Arapaho and Cheyenne Still Recovering from Sand Creek, Not Ready to Agree to Relinquish Land in Colorado

To accomplish the joint goals of reparations and removal, the U.S. sent a treaty delegation—led by Colonel Henry Leavenworth and including Colorado notables Kit Carson and William Bent—to the banks of the Little Arkansas River, where they arrived on October 4, 1865. There the party waited until several Cheyenne and Arapaho bands arrived on October 11, with their numbers eventually totaling more than 4,000. Among them were Black Kettle's Cheyenne and Little Raven's Arapaho—both of whom had been at Sand Creek—as well as five other Cheyenne bands and six other Arapaho bands.

On October 13, 1865, the surviving Arapaho and Cheyenne chiefs met with government commissioners. The Arapaho didn't want to agree on land at the time—few were present, the rest were up north. They were still reeling from the Sand Creek Massacre:

> Little Raven There is something very strong for us-that fool band of soldiers that cleared out our lodges, and killed our women and children. This is strong (hard) on us. ***There, at Sand creek, is one chief, Left Hand; White Antelope and many other chiefs lie there; our women and children lie there.*** Our lodges were destroyed there, and our horses were taken from us there, and ***I do not feel disposed to go right off in a new country and leave them.*** (Emphasis added).[86]

October 13, 1865: Treaty Council with Arapaho and Cheyenne - Unfortunately for You, Gold Discovered in Your Country

Treaty Council held in camp on the Little Arkansas River, October 13, 1865:

> We all fully realize that it is hard for any people to leave their homes and graves of their ancestors; but, ***unfortunately for you, gold has been discovered in your country, and a crowd of white people have gone there to live, and a great many of these people are the worst enemies of the Indians*** - men who do not care for their interests, and who would not stop at any crime to enrich themselves. These men are now in your country - in all parts of it - and there is no portion where you can live and maintain yourselves but what you will come in contact with them. The consequences of this state of things are that you are in constant danger of being imposed upon, and you have to resort to arms in self-defense. ... We want to give you a country that is full of game and good for agricultural purposes, and where the hills and mountains are not full of gold and silver. In such a country as this the government can fully provide for your wants ... We are sorry that we have bad people among us, as you are sorry that you have bad people among you; but this is unfortunately the case with all people, and however severe we make laws it is impossible to prevent crime. ***You may accede to our wishes, and be happy and prosperous, or you may refuse to make a treaty, and be ruined in health and happiness.*** (Emphasis added).[87]

October 14, 1865: Cheyenne and Arapaho Treaty Signed Removing Them from Colorado

The treaty which had been prepared was now read, article by article, by President Sanborn, and interpreted by John Smith to the Indians present. An article was submitted authorizing the Senate to make amendments without reference back to the Indians, but was objected to by the Indians, and withdrawn. The treaty was then signed by the commissioners and the chiefs and headmen of the Cheyenne and Arapaho tribes, and witnessed by the secretaries and other persons present, when the council adjourned. John R. Sanborn. President of the Commission.[88]

Article 6 of the Treaty of the Little Arkansas, 14 Stat. 703, negotiated on October 14, 1865, ratified May 22, 1866, and proclaimed February 2, 1867, provided for land and money reparations to survivors:

> The United States being desirous to express its condemnation of, and, as far as may be, repudiate the gross and wanton outrages perpetrated against certain bands of Cheyenne and Arapahoe Indians, on the twenty-ninth day of November, A.D. 1864, at Sand Creek, in Colorado Territory, while the said Indians were at peace with the United States, and under its flag, whose protection they had by lawful authority been promised and induced to seek, and the Government being desirous to make some suitable reparation for the injuries then done, will grant three hundred and twenty acres of land by patent, as well as individual payments for property lost.

This promise has not yet been kept. Descendants of those killed in the Sand Creek Massacre have been fighting for these lost reparations throughout the twentieth century and into the twenty- first.[89]

Little Arkansas Treaty - Land Specified for Reservation for Arapaho and Cheyenne in Indian Territory Already Given to Another Tribe

The Little Arkansas Treaty refers to a pair of treaties signed between the U.S. and Indian Nations in Kansas: one with the Southern Arapaho and Southern Cheyenne Nations and one with the Comanche and Kiowa. Of the two, the Treaty signed on October 14, 1865, with the Cheyenne and

Arapaho, was the most significant within Colorado because it removed the two Indian Nations to a new reservation in Indian Territory (present-day Oklahoma) and offered them reparations for the Sand Creek Massacre of the previous year. However, the U.S. had already removed other Indians to the same area and would have to move them to make space for the newcomers. Instead of issuing money to the individuals listed in the treaty for reparations, the Interior Department gave some of the money to the Nations and, in a common move, "returned the rest" to the Treasury as "surplus." Once money is returned to the Treasury it is final. The only method for securing money returned to the Treasury is by Congressional action—new legislation to appropriate monies is required.

January 1–February 2, 1865: Indian Military Campaign

After the Sand Creek Massacre of the Cheyenne and Arapaho on November 29, 1864, a number of Colorado and Kansas tribes allied to conduct hostilities against the U.S. Army and white settlers. Many of the Cheyenne survivors had fled north to the Republican River, where a large contingent of "Dog Soldiers" were camped.

Among the Cheyenne Indians one of the most important military societies was the Dog Soldiers, of which Tall Bull was chief. It was considered a great honor to belong to this band of warriors. In battle, a Cheyenne Dog Soldier would stake his dog rope in the ground. Dog ropes were made out of rawhide leather and decorated with porcupine quills and feathers. One end was tied to a red wooden stake. During combat, a Cheyenne Dog Soldier would plant the stake in the ground as a sign of perseverance and standing one's ground. The area over which the Dog Soldier could fight was limited to the length of the rope. Dog Soldiers would not remove the stake until their people had safely retreated or a comrade removed it, so it was used as a last resort.

On January 1, 1865, the Indians met at present-day St. Francis, Kansas, to plan a concerted strategy against the invasive settlement and trespass of white settlers on their land. In the meeting were the Cheyenne Dog Soldiers, the Northern Arapaho, and two Bands of Lakota Sioux, including the Brule, under Chief Spotted Tail, and the Oglala, under War Leader Pawnee Killer. The U.S. had failed to provide any protection of Indian lands and lives, affording military protection by Presidential Proclamation to the settlers, resulting in these Indians having to fight against insurmountable odds.

As many as 2,000 Cheyenne, Sioux, and Arapaho warriors shifted their camps closer to the South Platte River, where it cut through the northeast corner of Colorado. In the midst of this area was Fort Rankin (later Fort Sedgwick), an Overland Trail stagecoach station and the station town of Julesburg.

These warriors would lead a campaign between the 1st Battle of Julesburg on January 7, 1865 and the 2nd Battle of Julesburg on February 2, 1865, over a 150 mile stretch of the Overland Trail near the South Platte River in Northern Colorado.[90]

1865: Battle of Fort Rankin

On January 6, 1865, a small party of Indians hit a wagon train and killed 12 men. In the early morning hours of January 7th, the Indians attacked Fort Rankin. While the majority of the Indians concealed themselves in some sandhills a short distance from the Fort, Cheyenne Chief Big Crow and about ten of his warriors charged the Fort and then quickly retreated as a decoy. In response, Captain Nicholas O'Brien led a 60-man cavalry troop out of the Fort to chase the would-be attackers.

About three miles from the Fort, up to 1000 warriors were hidden in the nearby bluffs. Some Indian warriors fired prematurely, alerting Captain O'Brien. His troops fled back to the Fort with the Indians in pursuit, cutting off some of the soldiers before they reached safety. Of those who didn't reach the Fort, they dismounted to defend themselves. In the battle, 14 soldiers and four civilians were killed. Captain O'Brien and the rest of his men made it back to the Fort.

As the remaining troops prepared to defend the Fort against further attack, the Indians looted the stage station, store, and warehouse at Julesburg. Julesburg was only 200 miles east of Denver. It was an important waystation for immigrants and settlers traveling along the Platte River on the Oregon Trail, which built up around the home station for the Overland Trail

Stagecoach Lines.

In response to the attack on Fort Rankin, General Robert Byington Mitchell gathered 640 cavalry, a battery of howitzers, and some 200 supply wagons at Cottonwood Springs, which was located near present-day North Platte, Nebraska. He then marched southwest to find and punish the Indians who had attacked Fort Rankin and Julesburg. On January 19th, he found their deserted camp and returned to his base.

In the meantime, the Indians raided ranches and stagecoach stations up and down the South Platte River Valley. The Sioux struck east of Julesburg, the Cheyenne west of Julesburg, and the Arapaho in between. George Bent, the mixed-race son of William Bent, the founder of Bent's Fort, and his Cheyenne wife, was with this group of Indians. He would later say that at night "the whole valley was lighted up with the flames of burning ranches and stage stations, but the places were soon all destroyed, and darkness fell on the valley."

Just weeks after the first attack at Julesburg, the warriors returned in force on February 2, 1865, where they once again looted the town and, this time, burned it to the ground. They also looted some wagon trains. The 15 soldiers and 50 civilians sheltered at nearby Fort Rankin did not venture outside the Fort's walls. As the fire and smoke poured from the settlement, Captain O'Brien and 14 of his men, who had been away from the Fort, returned to Julesburg. O'Brien scattered the Indians with a round from his field howitzer, and the Indians fled.

1866: Governor Evans' Speech on Minerals, Agriculture Promoting Colorado

Colorado Governor Evans, in November 1866, remarked at a public meeting in Chicago:

> *I have just returned from visiting a district about one hundred miles by ten or fifteen in extent, lying across the main mountain range west of Denver City, which is pervaded throughout by extensive and rich veins of silver;* some are of pure silver ores, but the majority of them are argentiferous galena ores, varying in

richness, many of them yielding in the smelting furnace as high as six hundred dollars of silver to the ton of ore. Salinas, or extensive deposits of salt, are accessible, as in New Mexico; and even petroleum is found near the eastern base of the mountains. The forests supply timber even for exportation to Kansas, and the mountain streams are generally available for the uses of machinery and irrigation. The area of Colorado is 67,723,520 acres, and the most sanguine view of its future agriculture is comprised in a statement by Surveyor General Pierce, in 1866, that *"there are about 4,000,000 acres of agricultural land susceptible of irrigation, which will make productive farms."* (Emphasis added).

"The whole of the plains," according to the testimony of Governor Evans, "and the parks in the mountains of Colorado, are the finest of pastoral lands. Stock fattens and thrives on them the year round, large herds and flocks being kept there in the finest possible condition. In some parts, it is true, the snow covers the grass for a part of the winter, but in other places cattle and sheep are wintered without feeding, with entire success. The celebrated parks, North, Middle, South and San Luis, are fine agricultural valleys for grass and small grains."[91]

1866: Gold, Silver and Coal Discovered on Ute Land; Fertile Land, Timber, Water Power, All Requirements for Profitable Occupation

The Central Superintendency reported the following:

> Colorado Territory. *Last summer gold, silver, and coal were discovered in this section, which is reported to have many fertile valleys, abundance of timber and water powers, a fine climate, and all the requirements for profitable occupation. Many parties are preparing to invade this new land early in the spring* ... It is important that a treaty be made with the Grand River and Uintah bands at as early a day as possible. *I need scarcely allude to the necessity of limiting, as far as possible, the amount which the government will be called upon to pay for a cession* of the right of occupancy of the land by the Indians, but deem it of importance that, so far as possible, no promises of money annuities shall be made, but

that all payments shall be made in stock animals, implements, goods adapted to their wants, and for other beneficial objects. (Emphasis added).[92]

1867: American Express Co., Shoot Indians

Upper Arkansas Agency, Fort Larned, Kansas, May 27, 1867

Thomas Murphy, the Superintendent of Indian Affairs, on May 27 issued a complaint to his superior Commissioner Taylor. He wrote:

> "I have the honor to transmit herewith a circular issued by the superintendent of the American Express Company to their employes on the Smoky Hill route from Fort Harker to Denver City. I would call your attention particularly to the paragraph marked, viz: "If Indians come within shooting distance, shoot them; show them no mercy, for they will show you none."

> ... According to existing treaty stipulations the Cheyennes, Arapahos, and Apaches have permission to live in and roam over the country lying between these two rivers until the President orders their removal to reservations selected for them. If the government countenances these arbitrary acts of military commanders and superintendents of express companies in violating treaties, it is unreasonable to expect that the Indians will keep their part of these treaties. If this condition of affairs is permitted to exist much longer, every effort that has been made during the past two years by the civil officers of the government to promote peace and friendship among those Indians, and to prevent depredations, will have been utterly in vain, and it is but reasonable to expect that an Indian war of gigantic proportions will ensue, which will astonish the American people and cost millions of treasure. In view of these facts, I respectfully request that you will take such immediate steps as in your judgement will the soonest and most effectually put a stop to these arbitrary and cruel orders."[93]

1867: Central City Indian Scalp Bounty

The citizens of Central City have raised $5,000 to pay for Indian scalps, and offer $25 each for "scalps with the ears on."[94]

1867: Medicine Lodge Treaties - Cheyenne and Arapaho Treaty Establishing Reservation in Indian Territory

The Medicine Lodge Treaties in 1867 were a series of three treaties between the U.S. and the Comanche, Kiowa, Plains Apache, Southern Cheyenne, and Southern Arapaho nations. By treating with multiple tribes at once, the appointed Peace Commission's goal was to "establish security for person and property along the lines of railroad now being constructed to the Pacific." Leading the negotiations would be Acting Indian Affairs Commissioner Nathaniel G. Taylor, Senator John B. Henderson of Missouri, General William T. Sherman, and Christian reformer Samuel F. Tappan, among others. President Grant was pursuing a "Peace Policy," preferring cultural warfare over military campaigns.

The U.S. had the upper hand as the military had already established forts in the region, the tribes were fractured along lines of peace and warfare, and they needed annuities to survive, given the depletion of their subsistence base.

On October 28, the Cheyenne and Arapaho chiefs signed a treaty creating a reservation in western Indian Territory. Captain Barnitz of the 7th U.S. Cavalry, who recorded the speeches during the negotiations, expressed his misgivings.

> "They have no idea that they are giving up, or that they have ever given up the country which they claim as their own... *The treaty amounts to nothing*, and we will certainly have another war sooner or later with the Cheyennes, at least, and probably with the other Indians..." (Emphasis added).

The eastern plains of Colorado were cleared of Indians by 1870, primarily because superior military power and the physical removal to Indian Territory eliminated the presence of these peoples. Unlike the northern plains, there was no continual warfare between new-comers and Indians, nor was there inter-tribal squabbling. Colorado's Indians were simply overwhelmed by the 100,000 immigrants that poured across the plains in 1859, and small bands like the Arapaho were inundated.[95]

1868: Battle of Beecher Island

The Battle of Beecher Island was fought on Sep. 17, 1868, on the Arikaree River, near present-day Wray, Colorado. Fifty-one scouts and frontiersmen under the command of Colonel George A. Forsyth engaged the combined forces of the Northern Cheyenne, Arapaho, and Oglala after hunting them for several days due to their attacks on settlers. The advantage of the frontiersmen was a new firearm, the Spencer Seven repeating rifle; it shot seven times without re-loading. Unaware of this new rifle, the Indians tried making a direct charge on the frontiersmen, but were cut down. The frontiersman took cover on a sandbar island. The battle changed to a siege; starvation was the Indian plan. The frontiersmen lay in their sand pits for a whole week, drank river water, and ate horse meat. Two of their scouts were able to escape and go for help. Three military rescue parties departed following different routes due to the uncertainty of Forsyth's location. The Battle had the makings of a disaster until the Tenth Cavalry and other units arrived and routed the Indians.

1868: Ute Treaty of 1868 - Utes Cede Central Rockies

The Ute Treaty of 1868, also known as the "Kit Carson Treaty," was negotiated between agents of the U.S., including Kit Carson, and leaders of seven bands of Nuche living in Colorado and Utah. The treaty created for the Utes a massive reservation on Colorado's Western Slope in exchange for ceding the Central Rockies to the U.S. For the miners, it opened a huge portion of the mineral-rich Rocky Mountains to development. A reservation was created in northeast Utah for the Uintah Utes.

In 1870 Governor Edward M. McCook wrote a letter declaring:

> "I have never been able to comprehend the reasons which induced the Colorado officials and the General Government to enter into a treaty setting apart one-third of the whole area of Colorado for the exclusive use and occupation of the Ute nation." He claimed: "The greater part of this country is the best agricultural, pastoral, and mining land on the continent … The Ute reservation includes mines which will pay $100 per day to the man, grasses are luxuriant and inexhaustible, and a soil richer and more fruitful than any other in

the Territory." McCook closed his letter with an appeal to the ideals of Manifest Destiny: ***"I believe that God gave to us the earth, and the fullness thereof, in order that we might utilize and enjoy His gifts. I do not believe in donating to these indolent savages the best portion of my Territory."*** (Emphasis added).[96]

1869: Battle at Summit Springs

In response to a series of Cheyenne Indian raids in north-central Kansas in 1868 and 1869, after the Washita Massacre, Colonel Eugene Carr, with 244 men of the 5th U.S. Regiment of Cavalry and 50 Pawnee Scouts led by Major Frank North, were given orders to clear the Republican River country of all Indians. On July 11, 1869, Carr's force came upon an unsuspecting Cheyenne camp and attacked at 3 p.m., from three sides at once.[97]

Southern Cheyenne Chief Tall Bull along with Heavy Furred Wolf, Pile of Bones, Lone Bear, Black Sun, White Rock, Big Gip, Powder Face and 45 Cheyenne and Sioux men, women and children were killed at Summit Springs, near Sterling, Colorado, by the U.S. Cavalry. The Indian camp contained 84 lodges housing approximately 450 people. Even though the battle took place in the middle of the afternoon it came as a complete surprise to the Indians.[98]

The battle lasted nearly three hours. When the shooting finally stopped, around 6 p.m., a powerful prairie thunderstorm rolled in from the southwest and pummeled the battleground with rain and hail and everyone was forced to take cover wherever they could.

The diary of Major Frank North reads:

> "Sunday, July 11, 1869. Marched this morn at 6 A.M. with fifty of my men and two hundred whites, with three days' rations. Follow trail until three P.M. and came up to the village. Made a grand charge and it was a complete victory. Took the whole village of about 85 lodges. Killed about sixty Indians. Took seventeen prisoners and about three hundred ponies and robes, etc., innumerable. Rained pretty hard tonight."

By capturing the Dog Soldiers' village, many of the ponies, and practically all of their supplies and equipment, Carr's offensive effectively ended Cheyenne resistance on the Southern Plains.

One story told from the Battle is worth repeating:

> As the mounted horsemen galloped toward the hide-covered lodges a young boy, later identified as 12-year-old Little Hawk, was caught between the advancing Cavalry and the horses that he had been herding. The horses he was guarding were spooked by the advancing troops and began to scatter. Although the boy could have made his escape he mounted his own pony, gathered up the horses that had broken away and drove them into the camp ahead of the charging troops.... at the edge of the village he turned and joined a band of warriors that were trying to hold us back, while the women and children were getting away, and there he died like a warrior. No braver man ever existed than that 15 year old boy. His actions so impressed Captain Luther North that he recorded the events in his book "Man of the Plains."[99]

Mr. Clarence Reckmeyer visited the site of the battle with Captain Luther H. North, who took part in the Battle. The Battle of Summit Springs was the last important battle fought by Plains Indians on Colorado soil.

The lodges and all the contents of the village, except such articles as the soldiers desired to keep were burned. A footnote in Mr. Reckmeyer's article notes in part:

> On a plate opposite page 128 of Our Wild Indians, by R. I. Dodge, is shown a tobacco pipe the description of which reads: "Tall Bull's tobacco pipe, ornamented with feathers and scalp locks." Tall Bull was chief of a band of outlaw Cheyenne and Sioux. He was killed at the Battle of Summit Springs, Colorado. [N]early a wagon load of Indian trophies were hauled from the battlefield to Fort Sedgwick.

An anonymous Indian artist's sketchbook captured at Summit Springs, which portrays Indian life and war with the bluecoats, is now in the Colorado History Museum in Denver.

A joint resolution of the Nebraska legislature approved February 23, 1870, reads in part as follows:

> The thanks of the people of Nebraska are hereby tendered to Brevet Major General Carr and the officers and soldiers under his command of the 5th U.S. Cavalry, for their heroic courage and perseverance in their campaign against hostile Indians, driving the enemy from our borders and achieving a victory at Summit Springs, Colorado Territory. The thanks of this body and the people of the State of Nebraska are hereby also tendered to Major Frank J. North and the officers and soldiers under his command of the 'Pawnee Scouts' for the heroic manner in which they have assisted in driving hostile Indians from our frontier settlements.

A resolution adopted by the Colorado legislature on January 25, 1870, reads as follows:

> "Whereas, The prosperity of this territory has been greatly retarded during several years past by Indian warfare, preventing immigration, and greatly paralyzing industry; and whereas, defenseless women and children of our pioneer settlements have been murdered by savages, or subjected to captivity worse than death; and whereas, a detachment of U.S. troops under General Carr, on the twelfth [11th] of July last, at Summit Springs, in this territory, after a long and tedious pursuit, achieved a signal victory over a band of Dog Indians, retaking considerable property that had been stolen, and recapturing a white woman held captive. Resolved, That the thanks of the people of Colorado, through the council and house of representatives of the legislative assembly of the territory of Colorado, be extended to Brevet Major General Eugene A. Carr, of the U.S. Army, and the brave officers and soldiers of his command for their victory thus achieved. Resolved, That the secretary of the territory be required to have a copy of these resolutions prepared upon parchment, and transmitted to General Carr."[100]

1871: Indian Appropriations Act Ends Treaty-Making with Indian Nations

The 1871 Indian Appropriations Act ended treaty making with Indian Nations.

1872: Colorado Citizens Want 1868 Treaty Revised for Utes to Cede San Juan Mts. due to Silver Discoveries

By 1872, the discovery of silver in the San Juan Mountains of southwestern Colorado caused the settlers in Colorado to agitate for revision of the 1868 Ute Treaty. The Colorado delegation to Congress complained that this vast amount of land was underutilized by the lazy Ute people.

In 1872, a government commission consisting of Hon. John D. Long, General John McDonald and Governor E. M. McCook, was appointed, under a resolution of Congress introduced by Mr. Chaffee, with instructions to negotiate a treaty with the Ute Indians for a reduction of their immense reservation in the southwestern division of the Territory, and covering the rich mineral-bearing section known under the general term of the "San Juan country."

The commission came to Denver, went south to Fort Garland and thence to the Los Pinos agency beyond the San Juan Mountains. The councils embraced delegations from the Capote, Mouache, Winnemuche, Tabeguache, White River and Uintah bands. They brought with them a large quantity of goods to be distributed as inducements to favorable action. The terms proposed to the Indians were unsatisfactory to them, and the negotiations terminated in September.

In 1873, Felix Brunot, chairman of the Peace Commission, came out to exert his influence toward the conclusion of an accord. The Brunot Agreement was signed, cutting the San Juan region from the Ute lands. The area that the Utes controlled was still impressive—over 11,000,000 acres for a total population estimated at between four and six thousand.

At the outset the Indians were averse to surrendering any portion of their reservation, especially the agricultural valleys. Eventually, they agreed to cede, upon certain conditions, the area which included the principal mines.[101]

1873: San Juan Mountains - Richest Mining District

The country ceded by the Utes, including, as it does, probably the most extensive and richest mining district in the United States, embraces about four million acres of land, of very little value to Indians, being unfit for agricultural purposes and devoid of game, but of almost incalculable value to Colorado and the nation.[102]

1874: Brunot Agreement - Utes Cede Mineral Rich San Juan Mountains

Prospectors had entered the San Juan mountains and there discovered valuable mines of silver and gold, but as it was a part of the Indian reservation, they were in danger of conflicts with the savages.[103] As a result of the discovery of gold and silver, the treaty between the U.S. and the Utes of Colorado would be revised three times, accounting for each new mineral discovery.

The Brunot Agreement of 1873 was ratified by the U.S. in 1874, and is most often remembered by Utes as the agreement when their land was fraudulently taken away. The Utes were led to believe that they would be signing an agreement that would allow mining to occur on the lands located only in the San Juan Mountain area, the site of valuable gold and silver ore. About four million acres of land not subject to mining would remain Ute territory under ownership of the tribe. However, they ended up forcibly relinquishing the lands to the U.S.

With completion of the agreement, the San Juan Mountains saw a mining rush that resulted in many towns being established in 1874 and 1875, including Silverton. When the boundaries of the ceded lands were surveyed, the surveyor failed to exclude Uncompahgre Park, and it was quickly settled, much to the dissatisfaction of the Utes. Seeing the abundant farm and grazing land that surrounded the ceded territory, the Colorado citizenry became even more covetous of the Utes' land, making it only a matter of time before most of the Utes were forced from their Colorado homeland.

1876: Colorado Statehood

Colorado became a state in 1876.

1877: Stay Friendly with Utes

> Every day it becomes of higher importance that friendly relations should be maintained with the Utes, for it is in their power to stop, for a time at least, the development of the great San Juan mining district, which borders on the reservation. Los Pinos, Co., Agent W. D. Wheeler.[104]

Mining in southwestern Colorado was not of the placer-type that characterized early activity in the central Rockies. In order to effectively extract the mineral wealth in the mountains, lode mining techniques were essential. Lode deposits could only be recovered by skilled labor and technology. In milling, ore was crushed into sand and then washed over copper plates embedded with mercury, or simply into sluice boxes to recover the gold. It was relatively inefficient, with as little as 25 percent of the gold content recovered. The inefficiency came because milling is only a physical separation process and does not break the chemical bonds between the rock and gold. The result was a need for large machinery, a substantial labor force, smelters and transportation.

1877: Comanche Peace Treaty with Utes

In the 1700s the Ute and Comanche tribes began peace negotiations to ensure peace between two powerful tribal allies that reigned over the southwestern plains, however, peace talks were interrupted and a fifty-year war followed. Peace talks began again and in 1877 the Ute Comanche Peace Treaty was finalized. Representatives of the Comanche Tribe traveled to Ignacio, Colorado, to finalize the Ute Comanche Peace Treaty.

1877: Commissioner Recommends Removing All Indians in Colorado and AZ to Indian Territory to Facilitate Mining and Farming by Whites

Commissioner E. A. Hayt reported to the Secretary in 1877 that all Indians in Colorado and Arizona should be removed to the Indian Territory in what is now Oklahoma. Miners, in search of gold and silver, could claim lands without regard to Indian reservations established by the U.S. by treaty or legislative authority. He further stated that all of the arable land was required by white settlers and feeding them was of paramount importance.[105]

The Military and The Colorado Frontier, Marshall Sprague

> These "ignorant savages" were blocking all progress in Colorado mining progress, railroad progress, homestead progress, city-making progress, stage road progress-west of the Ute reservation line. That line ran along the 107th parallel from the New Mexico border for 240 miles north through the present site of Pagosa Springs, Gunnison, Aspen, Gypsum, Glenwood Springs and up to 20-Mile Park in the Yampa River area. All those future townsites and all the country west of them to the Utah border were in the Ute reservation.[106]

Colorado Petitions for Removal of All Utes

At this time, articles headlining "The Utes Must Go" were being prepared by members of the staff of Governor Frederick W. Pitkin. Pitkin was a former miner who used his wealth (acquired from a gold mine in the San Juan Mountains of Colorado) to influence the revision of the Ute treaty in 1873 and to become the first governor of Colorado on its statehood in 1876. His view of the Utes was an expression of the statewide view among whites that they were an impediment to the development of the richest part of the state and should be removed to the Indian Territories or elsewhere.

William Vickers, an adviser to the Governor, wrote in the Denver Tribune:

> Honorable N. C. Meeker, the well-known Superintendent of the White River Agency, was formerly a fast friend and ardent admirer of the Indians. He went to the Agency in the firm belief that he could manage the Indians successfully by kind treatment, patient precept and good example. But utter failure marked his efforts and at last he reluctantly accepted the truth of the broader truism that the only truly good Indians are dead ones.[107]

On February 4, 1878, the Colorado delegation introduced the first of three bills designed to remove the Utes from Colorado. House Resolution 351 was typical of the three. It empowered the Secretary of the Interior to negotiate with the Utes and "establish by law the extinguishment of title to their lands, removal from their present locations and consolidation on certain reservations."[108]

Early in 1879, an editorial in the Denver Times stated what had become obvious to most white Colorado residents. Since the 1873 Brunot Agreement, pressure had continued to mount for the removal of the Utes from Colorado.

> *"Either they [the Utes] or we go, and we are not going. Humanitarianism is an idea. Western empire is an inexorable fact. He who gets in the way of it will be crushed."* (Emphasis added).[109]

1879: Battle of Milk Creek and Meeker Incident - Utes Forced out of Colorado

Nathan C. Meeker, White River Ute Reservation Indian Agent, was the wrong person to appoint as the White River Indian Agent. He had no experience working with Indians and the White River Utes resented his paternalistic attitudes. He expressed his unfavorable opinions about the Utes in the press and to Nevada's popular Senator Teller:

> In an article in the *Greeley Tribune* on January 29, 1879, Meeker had written: "The habits of this sui generis [unique] American aristocracy seem almost identical with those of the European. Neither will work, neither attach any value to learning, both have the lower classes do work for them, both find occupation and happiness in gambling and horseracing, and the women in both are of no account."[110]

Captain Jack and thirteen other Utes went to see Governor Pitkin in Denver where they asked him to remove Meeker.[111]

Meeker believed the Indians must be brought down to the level of basic survival in order to guide them to civilized and agrarian lifestyles. He reported to Colorado's influential Senator Teller, "I propose to cut every Indian down to the bare starvation point if he will not work."[112]

Nathan Meeker wrote the following in an article published in the American Antiquarian Newsletter, 1878:

> "They are savages, having no written language, no traditional history,

no poetry, no literature... a race without ambition, and also a race deficient in the inherent elements of progress. Vermin abound on their persons..."

The Utes suspected him of direct involvement with the anti-Ute movement in the State.[113]

On Sep. 10, 1879, Meeker requested a telegram be sent to Commissioner Hayt requesting troops to repress a threatened uprising by the White River Utes after a Ute pushed him during an argument. The message reached Commissioner Hayt on Sep. 13, 1879. It was forwarded by Secretary of the Interior Carl Schurz to Secretary of War George W. McCrary, and ultimately received by General of the Army William T. Sherman. The location of the White River Agency was at the end of the Army's operational reach. General Sherman approved the request for troops and instructed the Commander of the Division of the Missouri, Major General Phillip H. Sheridan, to order "the nearest military commander" to send troops to White River.

The Commander of the Department of the Platte, Brigadier General George Crook, gave the following order to the forces at Fort Steele: You will move with a sufficient number of troops to White River Agency under special instructions. The special instructions that General Crook spoke of were to contact the agent on the scene and "develop" the situation. Major Thomas T. Thornburg began his march to the White River Agency on Sep. 22, 1879, with a total of 153 soldiers and 25 civilians.

On Sep. 25, 1879, Major Thornburgh wrote to Agent Meeker seeking instructions. Thornburgh continued his march toward the Agency. En route, a delegation of eleven Utes met with Thornburgh, voicing their concern over the arrival of troops and denouncing Agent Meeker.

On Sep. 27, 1879, Meeker sent a letter to Major Thornburgh:

> ...the Indians are greatly excited, and wish you to stop at some convenient camping place, and then that you and five soldiers of your command come into the Agency, when a talk and a better understanding can be had. ... ... ***The Indians seem to consider the***

advance of the troops as a declaration of real war. ... The first object is to allay apprehension. (Emphasis added).[114]

Major Thornburgh unilaterally decided that instead of sending a small group to meet with Meeker as Meeker and the Indians personally requested of him, he would enter the Reservation with all of his soldiers, fearing trouble. He sent Agent Meeker the following message:

> *I have, after due deliberation, decided to modify my plans* ... I shall move with my entire command to some convenient camp near, and within striking distance of your agency, reaching such point during the 29th. ... I have carefully considered whether or not it would be advisable to have my command at a point as distant as that desired by the Indians who were in camp last night, and have reached the conclusion that under my orders, which require me to march this command to the agency, I am not at liberty to leave it at a point where it would not be available in case of trouble. (Emphasis added).[115]

When Thornburgh's command reached Milk Creek, twenty-five miles from the agency, and within the Reservation, a large body of Indians confronted it ... For seven days, Thornburgh was besieged by the Utes. Major Thornburgh and thirteen of his men were killed.[116]

On the same day, other Utes attacked the Indian Agency, killing Agent Meeker, his 10 male employees and taking five women and children captive.

Troops proceeded to Colorado from all directions.

Sample News Headlines from Colorado Rocky Mountain News (1878-79)

1878

> 2 January "Indian Hostilities"
> 3 March "Utes on Rampage, Whites Fear Uprising"
> 5 March "Utes Kill Cattle on Snake River"
> 18 April "Ute Massacre in Pagosa Springs"

23 April "Rumors of Ute War"
28 April "Utes' Gold Locations Secret from Whites"
24 May "Utes Rebellious Through Neglect of Indian Bureau"
21 July "Movements of Ute Indians"
3 August "Utes Kill Joe McLane, Stockmen Seek Revenge"
1 September "Ute Uprising Feared in Grand County"
12 September "Utes in Trouble over Murder of Settlers"

1879

1 January "Utes Make Trouble in Middle Park"
27 June "Utes Threaten Miners in North Park"
9 July "Ute Hostile Attitude Excites State Officials"
16 July "Shall We Kill or Starve the Indians? [editorial]"
6 August "The Indians Must Go"
14 August "Utes Arrested and Charged with Arson"
10 September Letter to the editor from Meeker complaining of his treatment by the Utes

October 1879: Leadville Chronicle

[T]he savages are sweeping through the outlying settlements of the State, murdering miners and ranchmen ... Some man is needed who will out Chivington—some man who will duplicate Sand Creek... Murder is the Indian game. Give them enough of it.

1879: Governor Pitkin's Order: Bring in, Dead or Alive, All Hostile Indians

It was not until October 13, 1879, that the newspapers reported on the Agency incident. The headlines blazed, "A SCENE OF SLAUGHTER." Governor Pitkin denounced the attack in no uncertain terms, and incidentally pointed out that 12,000,000 acres could be opened with the removal of the Utes. [Frederick Pitkin, quoted in the Denver Daily News, October 13, 1879.] Herein lay the perfect opportunity to be rid of the Indians for good.[117]

The Governor mustered two companies of the Colorado militia: His War

Order No. 1 was to "bring in, dead or alive, all hostile Indians found off the reservation ... consider all Indians off the reservation hostile, and bring them in, dead or alive, and we will determine their docility afterward."[118]

In the view of Colorado citizens, the Utes were both dangerous and an impediment to progress. ... Pitkin commented to the press:

> "It will be impossible for the Indians and whites to live in peace hereafter ... This attack had no provocation and the whites now understand that they are liable to be attacked in any part of the state ... **unless removed by the government they must necessarily be exterminated.**" (Emphasis added).[119]

William Vickers, an adviser to the Governor, wrote in the Denver Tribune:

> The Utes are actual, practical Communists and the Government should be ashamed to foster and encourage them in their idleness and wanton waste of property. Living off the bounty of a paternal but idiotic Indian Bureau, they actually become too lazy to draw their rations in the regular way but insist on taking what they want wherever they find it. Removed to Indian Territory, the Utes could be fed and clothed for about one half what it now costs the government.

1880: Congressional Investigation - Battle of Milk Creek

One contemporary historian postulates that the Utes attack was "directly ascribable to the neglect and indifference of the Indian Bureau at Washington. *The time for the distribution of the annuities to the White River Utes had passed, and the Bureau at Washington calmly ignored the whole business." Flour, blankets, and other supplies sat in depots at Rawlins, Wyoming, and rotted.* (Emphasis added).[120] Meanwhile, the Indians went hungry and naked. Then they began to wander off the reservation and make reprisals upon the settlers.[121]

In a Congressional investigation, the ambiguity in whether the Army intended to attack the Utes was sharply questioned. The soldiers did not have a flag of truce with them, officer Cherry waved a hat to arrange a parley with the Indians. The Utes thought it was a signal to attack. The investigation found it was contentious since it was not a typical signal, such as using a white flag:

> By Mr. POUND:
> Q. Would the Indians have respected a flag of truce?
> A. I, of course, cannot say as to that. ... They did not respect what was intended as a flag of truce, this waving of my hat.
> Q. Would not the waving of a hat be as much a sign of war as of Peace? Might it not be so considered by them?
> A. I know nothing of their customs in that respect, but the manner of my men stopping and sitting there quietly on their horses, and my own attitude, looking right towards the Indians, and not towards my men, and waving my hat in a friendly manner-all these things considered, it seems to me that there was no possibility of such a mistake.
>
> By Mr. Errett:
> Q. If you were going out to hold a parley, wouldn't it have been more prudent for you to have taken a flag of truce along.
> A. Well, it might have been better, but still I don't think that it would have made any difference. Indeed, I don't know that I had such a thing as a white handkerchief about me. I think the only handkerchief I had was a silk one around my neck, and that was of a different color.
>
> By Mr. Poeiiler:
> Q. Was Mr. Meeker asked to come out with the command?
> A. Yes ....

Jack, a chief of the Utes, was recalled and further examined (through Ouray and another interpreter), as follows:

The soldiers when they got down to Milk River instead of stopping there as I thought they would, crossed the river ... they took the trail which led up to where the Indians were, and came up very fast until they got to a little creek there, and stopped on the north side of the creek ... About this signal that it was said the soldiers made I did not see any, but I understood that some Utes who were off quite a distance from me on the lower side saw some signal-saw a soldier take off his hat and wave it, but I did not see that, nor did anybody near me.[122]

1880: General Pope - Utes Worthless

The White River band of Utes is in no sense different from the other bands of that nation. They are worthless, idle vagabonds, who are no more likely to earn a living where they are by manual labor than by teaching metaphysics.[123]

Commissioner in Favor of Utes Removal to Utah

Thus, the Indian Bureau presented its desire to relocate the tribe as a matter of military and practical expediency. Commissioner Ezra A. Hayt stated:

> The reason I favored it [transfer of the Utes to Indian Territory] is this: The Indian Territory has enough fertile land to enable those Indians to settle down comfortably. It has a superabundance of fertile land. Again, the country is not broken, ridged, and labyrinthine like this region in Colorado; *it is a country where the Army could use artillery; and wherever our troops can use artillery the Indians know very well that it is useless for them to go upon the warpath*, so that, as a defensive measure, I think it would be wise to take them out of their fortresses and put them where they will be less formidable ... I think, then, if we wish to avoid expensive war and to save the lives of our soldiers, it is very desirable to put these Indians out of their fortresses in Colorado. (Emphasis added).[124]

A settlement was entered into that would lead to the forcible removal of the majority of the Utes from Colorado to Utah.

1880: After Thornburgh/Meeker Incidents Ute Delegation Forced to DC to Punish Them by Dispossessing Them of Their Reservation

Otto Mears accompanied Chief Ouray and an Indian delegation ordered to Washington, where an agreement was forced upon them. In order to punish the Indians for a massacre, dispossess them of their reservation, and remove them from Colorado, Congress passed the Act of June 15, 1880, 21 Stat. 199, which ratified and embodied an agreement by their leaders to cede to the U.S. all territory of "the present Ute Reservation," which would be restored to the public domain for sale. An Executive Order of 1882 restored the lands to the public domain.

The Southern Utes agreed to remove to and settle upon the unoccupied agricultural lands on the La Plata River, in Colorado … The Uncompahgre Utes agreed to remove to and settle upon agricultural lands on Grand River, near the mouth of the Gunnison River, in Colorado, if a sufficient quantity of agricultural land shall be found there, if not then upon such other unoccupied agricultural lands as may be found in that vicinity and in the Territory of Utah. The White River Utes agreed to remove to and settle upon agricultural lands on the Uintah Reservation in Utah.

It was proposed to settle the Uncompahgre Indians at the junction of the Uncompahgre and Grand River, in Colorado. The Ute commission questionably found that land at this point was unsuitable for the Indians, being neither adapted to agricultural nor pastoral pursuits; and removed said Uncompahgre Indians to the Territory of Utah.

1880: Utes Bribed to Sign Agreement to Cede Colorado Lands

The Utes at home refused at first to accept the legislation which would force their removal but were paid two dollars a piece by a commissioner, Otto Mears, to sign the Agreement. Commissioner Manypenny pressed bribery charges against Mears. Mears' hearing resulted in Interior Secretary Kirkwood agreeing to reimburse him for his personal expenses of $2,800 paid to the Indians. [Official documentation on allegations uncertain.]

As part of the Commission to select a site for the Uncompahgre Indians' new reservation, Mears gave the stipulations of the Ute Treaty a very "elastic" interpretation, and accordingly the Umcompahgre Utes were removed from Colorado to a reservation in eastern Utah. They thought they were going to be removed to Grand Junction. They had to be forcibly removed by the U.S. Army to Utah.

1880-1881: Commission Removes Utes

A commission was appointed to superintend the physical removal and settlement of the Utes: former Commissioner George W. Manypenny; Alfred B. Meacham of Washington, DC; John J. Russell of the Department of the Interior; John B. Bowman, a mining man from Kentucky; and Colorado's Otto Mears, mining and transportation promoter.[125]

1881: Forced Military Removal of 200 Miles

In late August 1881 the commissioners said it was time for the move to begin.

> Finally, with his troops surrounding the Ute camp, Brevet Brigadier General Mackenzie threatened that he would use force if necessary, and the sad cavalcade started down the Gunnison River at dawn on September l. ... they arrived at their destination on September 13, having accomplished the two hundred-mile journey in less than two weeks.

1881: Whites Pour onto Land Left by Utes with No Shred of Common Decency

General Pope wrote of the occasion:

> ... the whites who had collected, in view of [the Utes] removal were so eager and unrestrained by common decency that it was absolutely necessary to use military force to keep them off the reservation until the Indians were fairly gone ...[126]

The legislation cleared the way for the settlement of the valleys of the Gunnison, the Grand and the White Rivers. Throughout the state there was rejoicing. The Ouray Times said:

> Sunday morning the Utes bid adieu to their old hunting grounds and folded their tents, rounded up their dogs, sheep, goats, ponies and traps, and took up the line of march for their new reservation, followed by General McKenzie and his troops. This is an event that

has been long and devoutly prayed for by our people. How joyful it sounds, and with what satisfaction one can say, "The Utes have gone". The great menace to the advancement and development of this grand southwestern country is no more. Eastern people can now come to this section in the most perfect security. Besides it throws open to the dominion of white men one of the most fertile and beautiful valleys in all Colorado; a valley that will be to those who are so fortunate as to become owners of its broad acres, a happy land of Canaan.[127]

1881: Cattle Enterprises

Once the Utes were moved to Utah in 1881, the open range cattle industry expanded. As the U.S. forced the Cheyenne and Arapaho off their Colorado land, cattle could graze for free on thousands of acres. For a scant $10,000 investment, John Wesley Iliff soon became the largest landowner in northeast Colorado, with approximately 15,500 acres. Feeding his herds on the open range created an opportunity for large profits. While grazing on the range was free, buying land and appropriating water rights secured Iliff water along the South Platte River. He sold cattle to Indian reservations, army posts like Fort Laramie, the city of Cheyenne, and Union Pacific railroad construction crews in Nebraska, Wyoming and Utah. With refrigerated cattle cars, he could ship cattle and dressed beef to Chicago's Union Stockyards.[128]

1881: Legislative Assembly of Colorado Territory: Bill for an Act to provide for the Destruction of Indians and Skunks

John Coulter, a lawyer, justice of the peace, Territorial Legislator 1881, and Mayor of Georgetown in 1891 and 1892, introduced on January 29, 1881, in the Colorado House of Representatives, H.B. No. 178, a bill for an act to provide for the destruction of Indians and skunks. Section 1 provided as follows:

> Section 1: That any person who shall produce the scalp of any Indian or skunk found in this State, shall receive a reward or premium of twenty-five (25) dollars for each and every Indian or skunk scalp produced, to be paid out of the State treasury...

On February 2, 1881, the bill was referred to a special committee: H. Bill. No. 178, a bill for an act for the destruction of Indians and skunks, Was read a second time. Mr. Brush moved that the bill be referred to a special committee of five, with Mr. Coulter as chairman, Which motion prevailed.

On February 2, 1881, the special committee recommended that it be passed: The special committee to whom was referred H. B. No. 178, presented the following report: Mr. Speaker: Your special committee to whom was referred H.B. No. 178, a bill for an act for the destruction of Indians and skunks, have had the same under consideration, and instruct me to report said bill back to the House with the recommendation that it be passed. Jno. A. Coulter, Chairman.

On February 4, 1881, it was scheduled for a special order: H.B. No. 178, a bill for an act to provide for the destruction of Indians and skunks, and instruct me to report the same back to the House with the recommendation that it be made a special order for 7:30 P.M., February 11, 1881.

On February 11, 1881, it was moved that it be considered for final passage. The special order for this day and hour, being H.B. No. 178, a bill for an act in relation to Indians and skunks, Was taken up. Mr. Coulter moved that the bill be ordered engrossed and placed on its third reading and final passage. Mr. Lee moved that it be "chucked under the table," Which motion prevailed.[129]

1890: Commissioner Morgan - Southern Utes to Stay in Colorado

Colorado continued to advocate for removal to Utah of the one remaining Indian tribe in Colorado, the Southern Utes.

> The legislative assembly of [Utah] Territory at its last session adopted a memorial to Congress protesting against the proposed removal [of the Southern Colorado Utes] ... the presence of these Indians would be a menace and a hindrance to the settlement of the country... Utah has now her share of Indians, and should not be made to receive more at the selfish behest of a neighboring State.

They did not succeed and the Commissioner noted Colorado should not be too overly concerned:

> ... the Southern Utes are the only Indians now remaining in Colorado, and they number less than two thousand. Minnesota, Michigan, and Wisconsin each have over three times as many, Montana five, and California six times as many, North Dakota and South Dakota four and ten times as many, respectively, and the State of Washington five times as many; so that ***in the distribution of our Indian population, to those who regard their presence as a detriment, Colorado seems to have been much more fortunate than many of her sister States***. (Emphasis added).[130]

1895: Hunter Act - Opened Up Ute Strip to Homesteading and Sale

In 1895, the Hunter Act enabled lands within the Ute Strip to be allotted to tribal members, and the surplus lands homesteaded and sold to non-Indians. The Utes were divided. The Weenuchiu under the leadership of Chief Ignacio opposed allotment. They moved westward and settled near what is today Towaoc. The Southern Utes (Mouache and Caputa bands) agreed to allotment.[131]

1906: Mesa Verde Carved Out of Southern Ute Lands

The prehistoric relics of Mesa Verde were first brought to public attention in 1876 with the publication of the Hayden Surveys of 1874 and 1875-76.[132] Establishing a National Park was advocated.

> One of the main obstacles to the park was the fact that some of the most important cliff dwellings, including Cliff Palace, were not on public land, but within the Southern Ute Indian Reservation. In the spring of 1906 a survey was made by the Bureau of American Ethnology, with the help of Edgar Lee Hewett, to fix the park boundaries. Hewett accompanied the surveyors and identified the ruins to be included. As thus described, the proposed Mesa Verde park comprised a strip of land along the Mancos River fourteen and a half miles long and several miles wide, embracing a total area exceeding sixty-five square miles. Concerned over important omissions from

> the park proposal, Hewett wrote Commissioner Francis E. Leupp of the Office of Indian Affairs and suggested an amendment to Hogg's bill providing that all prehistoric ruins situated on Indian lands within five miles of the boundaries of Mesa Verde National Park also be included within the jurisdiction of its officers for administrative purposes. This strip contained an additional 274 square miles. The amendment was promptly accepted by the House Public Lands Committee. As Hewett wrote, "This secures what has been so much desired by all namely the inclusion of all the great Mesa Verde and Mancos Canyon ruins within the National Park."[133]

On June 15 the House Committee on Public Lands reported the Mesa Verde National Park bill favorably, and eight days later it had passed both the House and Senate. It was signed by President Roosevelt on June 30, only twenty-two days after he approved the Antiquities Act.[134]

> An Act Creating the Mesa Verde National Park SEC. 3. That the Secretary of the Interior be, and he is hereby, authorized to permit examinations, excavations, and other gathering of objects of interest within said park ... undertaken only for the benefit of some reputable museum, university, college, or other recognized scientific or educational institution, with a view to increasing the knowledge of such objects and aiding the general advancement of archaeological science. Approved, June 29, 1906.[135]

> According to the agreement with the Wiminuche, the government would obtain 12,760 acres on the Southern Ute Indian Reservation and agree to give the Indians a tract lying west and within the park boundary containing about 6,000 acres and a second tract.[136]

Colorado Moguls: Mining and Real Estate

Spencer Penrose came from a very accomplished eastern family; his brothers were a U.S. senator and Republican Party leader, a noted geologist, and a successful medical doctor. Penrose came west and as a businessman, miner, mill owner, and investor who worked primarily in the Pike's Peak region, he built up the city of Colorado Springs. He had assets in Colorado, Utah, Arizona, and Kansas, including mines and real estate properties. He is most notable for owning the Cash On Delivery mine in Cripple Creek and for building the Broadmoor Hotel.

In 1902, with the Cripple Creek gold rush slowing down, Spencer Penrose and Charles L. Tutt, Sr., along with the Guggenheims, invested in the speculative technology for extracting copper from low-grade ore proposed by Daniel Jackling, a mineralogist. The Bingham Canyon Mine in Utah started with underground mining and switched to open-pit mining, using steam shovels, with railway access to transport the ore for processing. It produced about 30 percent of all the copper used by the Allied Forces for weapons, equipment, tools, and communication wires. One of the largest man-made excavations on earth, it is visible from outer space. In 2013, it reached a width of 2.5 miles and a depth of 3,900 feet. Still in operation, it has produced more copper than any other mine in the world.

With his immense fortune, Penrose contributed to virtually every prominent landmark in Colorado Springs. Penrose built the world-famous Broadmoor Hotel, the Pike's Peak Highway, the Cheyenne Mountain Zoo, and the Will Rogers Shrine. He also started the Pike's Peak Hill Climb and along with his wife, Julie, was central in the founding of the Colorado Springs Fine Arts Center, the rejuvenation of Central City Opera, and the expansion of Colorado College. His philanthropy is continued through the El Pomar Foundation.

Metal Processing Enterprises[137]

Nathaniel Peter Hill (1832-1900) was a mining entrepreneur and U.S. senator from Colorado. In the 1860s, Hill, an accomplished chemist and metallurgist, bought mining interests in Black Hawk and developed the first successful smelter in Colorado, revolutionizing the mining industry in the fledgling territory and beyond. Hill recognized that Colorado's gold miners needed a new extraction method. In 1867, he founded the Boston and Colorado Smelting Company, opened Colorado's first successful smelter in January 1868. In the decade before Hill's smelter opened, miners in Gilpin County had extracted a total of $9.4 million in gold. In the decade after Hill's smelter opened, Gilpin County miners more than doubled their gold production to $20.2 million. Hill's company ruled Colorado's smelting industry in those years, and Hill also acquired mining interests in Central City. He was a friend of President Hayes and served as a U.S. Senator.

After his move to Denver, Hill expanded his business interests. He acquired real estate and helped develop property around the growing city. In 1887 he helped form the Denargo Land Company and served as its president. He also served as president of the United Oil Company and purchased a local newspaper, the Denver Republican. In his later years, he sat on the board of trustees of the Colorado School of Mines, where he also taught classes.

With the usual social congregation of the wealthy, his neighbors included the Evanses, Iliffs and the Byers. Byers owned the Rocky Mountain News and fifteen years after the Sand Creek Massacre still believed that Sand Creek had "saved Colorado and taught the Indians the most salutary lesson they ever learned."[138] This led to financial and political leverage, along with the consolidation and integration of common industrial interests.

Meyer Guggenheim made his fortune (one of the largest of the 19th century) through business ventures in mining and smelting, mostly in the U.S. After investing in silver mines in the Leadville mining district of Colorado, he expanded into ore smelting in Colorado. He built a number of smelters across the U.S. and in northern Mexico. Later, he expanded into copper (Utah's Bingham Canyon, Canada and Chile) and lead—needed in telephone and electrical systems. Internationally, he engaged in rubber and diamond production in the Belgian Congo.

City Developers, Denver, Colorado

Early arrivals such as Walter Cheesman, David Moffat, and James Archer led efforts to bring reliable and safe water service to Denver. They provided the financing for constructing and maintaining extensive ditch systems.

In 1868 Cheesman, John Evans and David H. Moffat began work to build the Denver Pacific Railroad to Cheyenne, Wyoming. Cheesman was president of the railroad for several years. He planned for the construction of the Union Station, and he was active in the building of the Denver Boulder Valley Railroad and South Park Road. The railroad helped Denver become a major city. He also was a director of the Denver, Northern, and Pacific Railway Company. Cheesman was an organizer of the International Trust Company and served as a member of its executive committee for more than 15 years, and he was a member of the Denver Real Estate Exchange. He bought real estate throughout the years, established financial institutions, and helped develop mines.

In 1870, he became a principal in a company to provide water to Denver. With David Moffat and Thomas Hayden, they consolidated two water plants into the monopolistic Denver Union Water Company in 1894, which grew to a $25 million organization. Cheesman built dams, reservoirs, and filtration and distribution systems.

City Developers, Durango, Colorado

General William J. Palmer, president of the Denver & Rio Grande Railway railroad, along with William A. Bell and John A. Porter formed the Durango Trust to establish the town site and buy and sell property. As investors in the New York and San Juan Mining and Smelting Company, they built a smelter in Durango, purchased a limestone quarry and several nearby coal mines. On July 8, 1882, the Denver & Rio Grande Railroad made its way into Silverton. In that year, the "Silvery San Juan" produced $20,000,000 worth of ore.

Investment Banking

Jay Cooke was an American financier who helped finance the Union war effort during the Civil War and the postwar development of railroads in the northwestern U.S. He is generally acknowledged as the first major investment banker in the U.S. and creator of the first wire house firm. On January 1, 1861, just months before the start of the American Civil War, Cooke opened the private banking house of Jay Cooke & Company in Philadelphia. Soon after the war began, the state of Pennsylvania borrowed $3,000,000 to fund its war efforts.

In the early months of the war, Cooke worked with Treasury Secretary Salmon P. Chase to secure loans from the leading bankers in the Northern cities. Cooke's own firm was so successful in distributing Treasury notes that Chase engaged him as special agent to sell the $500 million in "five-twenty" bonds—callable in five years and matured in 20 years— authorized by Congress on February 25, 1862. The Treasury had previously tried and failed to sell these bonds. Promised a sales commission of 0.5 percent of the revenue from the first $10 million, and 0.375 percent of subsequent bonds, Cooke financed a nationwide sales campaign, appointing about 2,500 sub-agents who traveled through every northern and western state and territory, as well as the Southern states as they came under control of the Union Army. Meanwhile, Cooke secured the support of most Northern newspapers, purchasing ads through advertising agencies, and often working directly with editors on lengthy articles about the virtues of buying government bonds. His editorials, articles, handbills, circulars, and signs most often appealed to Americans' desire to turn a profit, while simultaneously aiding the war effort. Cooke quickly sold the $500 million in bonds, and $11 million more. Congress immediately sanctioned the excess.

Cooke influenced the establishment of national banks, and organized a national bank at Washington and another at Philadelphia almost as quickly as Congress could authorize the institutions.

In the early months of 1865, the government faced pressing financial needs. After the national banks saw disappointing sales of "seven-thirty" notes, the government again turned to Cooke. He sent agents into remote villages and hamlets, and even into isolated mining camps in the west, and persuaded rural newspapers to praise the loan. Between February and July 1865, he disposed of three series of the notes, reaching a total of $830,000,000. This allowed the Union soldiers to be supplied and paid during the final months of the war. In 1870 his firm financed the construction of the Northern Pacific Railway.

Colorado Gold Production History

The total Colorado production of the precious and allied metals from 1859 to 1870, inclusive, was: Gold $27,213,081; silver $330,000; copper $40,000; total, $27,583,081.

The annual gold output of the state increased from $4,150,000 in 1890 to $28,702,036 in 1900.

A study by the U.S. Geological Survey in 1923 is very specific as to the value of minerals in Colorado. Even though it was written in 1923, an extrapolation of current monetary values can be made from this past data.

This history of mining in Colorado will be useless unless the facts set forth for the period 1859-1923 can point in some way to the future. That Colorado has been a large producer of metals is definitely known. That it has been chiefly a producer of gold and silver is shown by the fact that of the calculated gross value of recovered gold, silver, copper, lead, and zinc, amounting to $1,531,000,000, $673,000,000 in gold, or 44 per cent of the total, and 628,850,000 ounces of silver, with a commercial value of $501,734,000, or 33 per cent, represent the gold and silver added to the world's supply. Thus 77 per cent of the total gross value of Colorado's production of these five metals is represented by gold and silver. Most of the gold is still in existence. A great part of the silver was coined and in this form represents a value of $1.29 an ounce. The copper produced, chiefly as a by-product of gold and silver mining, amounting to 263,000,000 pounds, with a gross calculated value of $40,328,000, has not all been dissipated. The enormous quantity of lead recovered, 4,200,000,000 pounds, with a gross value of $189,662,000, and the large quantity of zinc recovered, 1,740,000,000 pounds, with a gross calculated value of $126,216,000.

It seems hardly a mere coincidence that the total gross value of these five metals-$1,531,000,000 to the end of 1923, is very close to the assessed valuation of the State of Colorado for 1923, $1,550,000,000. The fact that the curve of the assessed value from the early days of Colorado-when mining or labors dependent on mining had developed the only assessable wealth to the present time not only parallels but actually coincides with the curve of the gross production of the five metals cannot be a mere accident. Denver in particular owes its growth to mining. Colorado Springs owes a great part of its development to mining. Pueblo owes its industrial existence to mining and metallurgy.[139]

Colorado's gold output through 1965 was about 40,776,000 ounces.[140]

Other minerals and commodities currently mined in the state include oil, natural gas, coal, carbon dioxide, helium, molybdenum, sand, gravel, quarry aggregate, clay, limestone, gypsum, nahcolite (sodium bicarbonate), and dimension and decorative stone (e.g., marble, sandstone).[141]

Colorado's Mining Millionaires

By 1892, there were thirty-nine millionaires in Colorado. This article is set forth in its entirety. Many of these men had made their fortunes through mining or by supporting the development of mining in the state.

Official statistics show that Colorado produced from 1859 to December 31, 1904 at the current market prices for the metals: Gold $355,014,347; silver $386,457,857; lead $121,118,146; copper $17,835,820; zinc (a recent product) $10,740,207; total, $891,259,375.

The total Colorado production of the precious and allied metals from 1859 to 1870, inclusive, was: Gold $27,213,081; silver $330,000; copper $40,000; total, $27,583,081.

The annual gold output of the state increased from $4,150,000 in 1890 to $28,702,036 in 1900.

Note that this list does not include those millionaires who later benefited from the Cripple Creek gold boom of the 1890s. The average mine worker earned $3.00 per day in 1892.

There are few who have any idea of the number of millionaires in Denver and in Colorado. One would hardly believe that there are thirty-three … in this city. Besides there are six millionaires in the state outside of Denver. [Horace] Tabor heads the list with several millions, all made in mining.
Then comes [Nathaniel] Hill, whose money was made in the mining [and smelter] business…
David Moffatt accumulated his money in the banking and railroad business…
E. Eildy is another mining and smelting man. Charles Kountze…is in mining.
William James accumulated his wealth in the same business. John Reithmann is also in the mining business.
Samuel Morgan was a miner.
Jerome Chaffee was in the mining business.
H.M. Griffin of Georgetown was also a miner.

John W. Mackey, Comstock, from 1880 to 1888 owned and operated the Freeland mine, Clear Creek County, Colorado, which during his ownership produced $3,350,000 worth of mineral, mostly gold, within 600 feet from the surface.

The late L. Z. Leiter, of Chicago, and the late William H. Stevens, of Detroit, were the principal owners in the famous Iron Silver mine at Leadville. This mine since 1879 ... has produced upwards of $15,000,000 and is still paying dividends.

The late M. Guggenheim, of New York, ... and Charles Graham, of Philadelphia, made large fortunes out of their joint ownership and operation of the phenomenal A.Y. & Minnie mine at Leadville, which since 1870 has produced upwards of $8,000,000 from a comparatively small area and is still producing. ...

N.K. Fairbank, of Chicago, the late Charles D. Arms, of Youngstown Ohio; Robert McCurdy, also of Youngstown, Ohio, and D.M. Hyman, of Cincinnati, Ohio, made large sums out of the bonanza silver mines of Aspen in the '80s.

The late Joseph Reynolds (often known as "Diamond Joe"), of Chicago and St. Louis, made a large portion of his fortune from various mines in Clear Creek County.

The late Edmund C. Bassick ...made a handsome fortune out of the Bassick mine, Custer county, Colorado, and died a few years ago in his native state, Connecticut.

R. G. Shannon, of New York, is a large stockholder in the Portland mine, Cripple Creek, which produced from 1894 to December 31, 1904, $20,679,363 worth of gold and paid $5,377,080 in dividends.

Among the millionaire Colorado mining men now deceased were the following:

Ex-Senator H.A.W. Tabor made a large fortune from various mines in Leadville...

W.S. Stratton made his fortune in the 90s in the famous Independence mine, Cripple Creek ... In 1894 Winfield Scott Stratton became the first millionaire to come out of the District.

William Church made a large fortune in the 90s in copper mines in Graham county, Arizona ...

Among the Colorado men who made fortunes by mining in Colorado and are not now residents of the state are the following:

Eben Smith, now resident in Los Angeles, Calif., during a period of over 30 years mined successively in Gilpin and Boulder counties and at Leadville, Aspen and Cripple Creek. He was known as the "Dean of Mining." He was a mine owner, smelting company executive, railroad executive and bank owner.

Thomas F. Walsh, now resident in Washington, DC, made his fortune in the 90s and since out of the famous Camp Bird mine, near Ouray.

D.R.C. Brown, Jerome B. Wheeler and W.B. Devereux, all now residents in New York city, made handsome fortunes out of mining at Aspen in the 80s.

J.J. Hagerman, now resident in the Pecos valley, New Mexico, derived a considerable part of his fortune from mining in Aspen.

Henry R. Wolcott, still a resident of Denver, but mostly resident in New York city, profitably mined at Leadville, Creede and Cripple Creek, Colorado, also in Montana and is now mining in New Mexico.

Edward G. Stolber, now traveling around, made a fortune out of the Silver Lake mine, near Silverton, Colorado.

William Bailey and O.P. Posey, both resident at Los Angeles, Calif., each made very considerable sums out of the famous Boy mine near Telluride.

Partial list of present residents of Denver alone ... who have individually made anywhere from $50,000 up to millions of dollars from mining operations ... does not include any "professional promoter" or "company-monger" ... [Similar lists could be made of residents in Colorado Springs, Pueblo, or elsewhere.]

Frank Adams, (Telluride); Charles Armstrong, (Ouray); A. Ashbaugh, M.D., (Gilpin county).

William Barth, (Cripple Creek); T. Walter Beam, (Telluride);

J.W. Benson, (Ouray); John Best (Gilpin county); Max Boehmer, M.E., (Leadville); Charles Boettcher, (Leadville); Henry Boltholf, (Leadville); S.G. Bonney, M.D., (Cripple Creek); James J. Brown, (Leadville); L.B. Brown, (Leadville);

W. G. Brown, Banker, (Leadville); D.W. Brunton, (Aspen); Charles Burns, (Aspen, Creede); Hugh Butler, attorney, (Gilpin county, Aspen, Leadville); W.H. Bryant, attorney (Creede).

F.J. Campbell, (Cripple Creek, Colorado, Goldfield, Nev.);

L.E. Campbell (Leadville, Creede, Cripple Creek); John F. Campion, (Leadville, Breckenridge); Rodney Cavanaugh, (Creede); Charles Cavender, attorney, (Leadville); Walter S. Cheeseman, (Leadville, Creede, Cripple Creek, Red Cliff);
A.J. Clark, (Telluride); Judge E.A. Colburn, (Cripple Creek); Edward Collingwood, (Breckenridge); T.T. Cornforth, merchant, (Black Hills, S.D.); E.B. Costigan (Telluride).

Thomas F. Daly, insurance, (Leadville); W.H. Davis, (Cripple Creek); Royal J. Donnen, (Leadville); D.H. Dougan, banker, (Leadville); James Doyle, (Cripple Creek and La Plata county); John Dumont, (Clear Creek county).

James H. Emerson, (Cripple Creek); Augustus L. Engelbach, (Leadville); Robert Esty, (Leadville).

John B. Farish, M.E., (Old Mexico); Charles Finding, (Breckenridge);

Michael Finnerty, (Leadville, Cripple Creek); John Fortune, (Park county); E. Le Neve Foster, M.E., (Georgetown and Summit county); Peter J. Fredericks, (Cripple Creek); W.A. Fullerton (Gilpin county).

J. Gavin, (Leadville); Judge L.M. Goddard, (Leadville); Timothy Goodwin, (Leadville); J.W. Graham, M.D., (Cripple Creek, Colorado, Goldfield, Nev.); Horace Granfield, (Cripple Creek); ex-Governor James B. Grant, (Leadville).

Percy Ham, (Leadville); Charles Harker, (Gilpin county); E.H. Hendrie, merchant, (Leadville); Charles. L. Hill, (Leadville); George Hook, (Leadville); B.A. Hopkins, (Georgetown and Summit county); Charles J. Hughes, attorney, (Aspen, Cripple Creek); Albert E. Humphreys, (Creede).

Harry C. James, (Leadville).

Silas S. Kennedy, (Boulder county); E.A. Kent, manufacturer, (Hinsdale county); Benjamin Kimber, (Gilpin county); Charles B. Kounizo, banker, (various districts).

Judge Owen Le Fevre, (Creede); Lewis E. Lemen, M.D., (Clear Creek County); W.R. Leonard, (Coeur d'Alene, Idaho); Henry P. Lowe, (Gilpin county).

A. P. Mackoy, (Aspen, Cripple Creek); Alfred Mann, M.D., (Arizona); James McClurg, (Cripple Creek); Governor Jesse F. McDonald, (Leadville); Robert L. Martin, (Clear Creek and Gilpin counties); D.G. Miller, (Ouray, Creede, Aspen); David H, Moffat, Jr., banker, (Leadville, Creede, Aspen); John. G. Morgan, (Leadville, Creede).

Samuel D. Nicholson, (Leadville, Lake City).

T.J. O'Donnell, attorney, (Hinsdale county); Harper M. Orahood, (Gilpin county); Judge Frank W. Owens, (Leadville).

W. Bryd Page, M.E, (Leadville); A.D. Parker, general auditor, Colorado and Southern railroad system, (Tonopah and Goldfield, Nev.); Charles C. Parsons, attorney, (Leadville, Colorado, Utah); Henry M. Porter, (New

Mexico, Arizona); John A. Porter, (Telluride); Thomas H. Potter, banker, (Gilpin county).

Albert H. Reynolds, (Aspen, Ouray, etc.); Link Reynolds, (Leadville); W.O. Reynolds, (Leadville); August Riche, (Leadville); J.H. Robeson, (Georgetown); Julius Rodman, (Creede, Lake City, Leadville); R.T. Root, (Arizona, New Mexico, etc.); ex-Governor John L. Routt, (Leadville).

Jacob F. Sanders, (Creede); Otto Sauer, (Gilpin County); D.J. Sayer, (Telluride, Colorado, Arizona); Hal Sayre, (Gilpin county); T.S. Schlesinger, (Leadville); Dennis Sheedy, banker, (Leadville); Fred L. Sigel, (Cripple Creek, Colorado, Goldfield, Nev.); Michael E. Smith, (Leadville); Link Spangler, (Cripple Creek); J. Standley, (Gilpin county); H.C. Stuchfield, manufacturer, (Hinsdale county); Dennis Sullivan, (Gilpin county, Leadville and Cripple Creek, Colorado, Arizona and Old Mexico); S.J. Sullivan, (Leadville, Colorado, Old Mexico); William Sullivan, (Silverton, Ouray); David Swickhelmer (Rico, Telluride).

Willard Teller, attorney and his brother, U.S. Senator Henry M. Teller, (Gilpin and Boulder counties); Joseph A. Thatcher, banker, (Gilpin county); ex-Governor Charles S. Thomas, (Leadville, Aspen, Creede); Judge C.I. Thomson, (Leadville, Aspen, etc.).

W.S. Ward, (Leadville); Joseph Watson, (Georgetown); Frank G. White, (Leadville); Edward W. Williams, (Gilpin and Clear Creek counties); R.R. Williams, (Gunnison county); G.S. Wood, (Cripple Creek, Colorado, Goldfield, Nev.); Lee Wood, (Rico, Cripple Creek).

W.H. Yankee, (Aspen, etc., etc.).

Adolph J. Zang, brewer, (Cripple Creek, Ouray).

All present indications are that during 1905 Colorado will equal, if not exceed, her greatest past annual record production of the precious and allied metals. viz, that of 1900, which was $50,314,010; also, that Colorado will continue to produce annually from $40,000,000 to $50,000,000 worth of the precious and allied metals for many years yet to come.[142]

Colorado Counties

All of today's 64 Colorado counties have a history of Indian occupation. On November 1, 1861, the new Colorado Territory created 17 original counties: Arapahoe, Boulder, Clear Creek, Costilla, Douglas, El Paso, Fremont, Gilpin, Guadalupe, Huerfano, Jefferson, Lake, Larimer, Park, Pueblo, Summit, and Weld. It is important to understand that these counties initially covered immense areas and were later reduced in size. For example, seven counties now occupy the area originally assigned to Weld County.

The comprehensive research done by History Colorado and Colorado Encyclopedia has been invaluable in understanding the many counties of Colorado. See Appendix 1 for Chart of Counties.

"A Book of Christian History Bound in the Flayed Skin of an American Indian"

> In 1893, **Iliff School of Theology was gifted a book of Christian history bound in the flayed skin** of a murdered Lenape man. It was on display from 1893 to 1974. (Emphasis added).[143]

Lenape Indians

The Lenape, also known as the Delaware, were originally an Eastern Woodland Indian Nation located in present-day New Jersey, Pennsylvania and the Delaware River watershed. See reference: 2000 Rees, Mark A., Gina S. Powell, and Neal H. Lopinot. Delaware Town Archaeological Survey and site assessment in the James River Valley of Christian County, Missouri, Center for Archaeological Research Report No. 1081/1109.[144]

Today, there are three federally recognized tribes in the U.S., including, the Delaware Nation, Anadarko, Oklahoma; the Delaware Tribe of Indians, Bartlesville, Oklahoma; and the Stockbridge-Munsee Community, Bowler, Wisconsin. In Canada, there are the Munsee-Delaware Nation; the Moravian of the Thames First Nation; and the Delaware of Six Nations.

Disturbing Content

The Rocky Mountain Public Television recorded the Convening of Lenape Elders in April 2022 and the Iliff School of Theology leadership regarding this book and produced a documentary video of the event which is online. It is extremely powerful.[145]

At the outset of the video, the Rocky Mountain Public Television stated the following:

> Tonight's program contains language that may not be suitable for all audiences. Viewer discretion is advised. This warning is to allow our viewers the space to prepare for this content.
>
> Information and education in history's raw and brutal past must be acknowledged and heard as we move forward to accountability and healing.[146]

It is true here.

John Wesley Iliff, Cattle Baron

John Wesley Iliff, the namesake of the Iliff School of Theology, made his fortune during the cattle boom of the later 1860s and 80s, in Wyoming and Colorado.

Wyoming's Cattle Industry Includes Iliff

In his article, The Wyoming Cattle Boom, 1868-1886, Samuel Western described it all:

> *An 1879 Report of the Commissioner of Indian affairs reported that the federal government bought 11,311 head of cattle from ranchers in 1878 alone to distribute to various western tribes.*
>
> Stockmen fanned out across Wyoming Territory, staking out ranches in the Bighorn Basin, the Powder River Basin and the upper **Green River Valley.** Cattle kept pouring in from Texas and Oregon.

Outside capital flooded in as well. Wholesale prices for cattle reached a heart-stopping $6.47 per hundredweight in May 1870— meaning an 850-pound steer went for $55. Those already in the cattle business around Cheyenne and Laramie—the Lathrams, the Iliffs and the Dole brothers— made a killing. Investors were convinced that they, too, could repeat such profits.

The math *was* pretty compelling. According to Scottish-born writer, cattleman and Wyoming ranch manager John Clay, it cost about $1.50 to raise a range steer. There were marketing and shipping charges, certainly, but during an unheated market, you sold that same steer for $23.00; at the peak it sold for over $60.00 per head. A stockman could enjoy a net profit of $40.00 per head during good times. ...

Prominent historian of the American West W. Turrentine Jackson estimates that British interests invested more than $45 million in American cattle in the 1880s. Between 1880 and 1900, 181 livestock companies incorporated in Wyoming with an aggregate capitalization of $94,095,800.

In 1882, the six counties of Wyoming reported 476,274 cattle, worth nearly $7 million, on their tax rolls. Since, for tax reasons, many cattlemen were known for underestimating their herds, there may have been twice that number on the range. (Emphasis added).[147]

Colorado's Cattle Enterprises Includes Iliff

Once the Utes were moved to Utah in 1881, the open range cattle industry expanded. As the U.S. forced the Cheyenne and Arapaho off their Colorado land, cattle could graze for free on thousands of acres. For a scant $10,000 investment, John Wesley Iliff soon became the largest landowner in northeast Colorado, with approximately 15,500 acres. Feeding his herds on the open range created an opportunity for large profits. *While grazing on the range was free, buying land and appropriating water rights secured Iliff water along the South Platte River. He sold cattle to Indian* *reservations*, army posts like Fort Laramie, the city of Cheyenne, and Union Pacific railroad construction crews in Nebraska, Wyoming and Utah. With refrigerated cattle cars, he could ship cattle and dressed beef to Chicago's Union Stockyards. (Emphasis added).[148]

1934 Rocky Mountain News Article: "An Indian Warrior's Skin, Finer Than The Finest Vellum, Forms The Binding Of An Ancient Book, 'The History Of Christianity,' One Of The Most Treasured Relics In The Library Of The Iliff School Of Theology"

In 1934, an article was written in the Rocky Mountain News about the Iliff School of Theology's celebrated book, "The History of Christianity, published in Latin in Europe in the 1700s. It contained a note: "This Latin church history book ... is bound in American Indian skin. The Indian was killed in hand-to-hand combat by General David Morgan of Morgantown, West Virginia, on April 1, 1779." (Underlined text emphasized in original document). The newspaper article went on to state:

> *"An Indian warrior's skin, finer than the finest vellum, forms the binding of an ancient book, 'The History of Christianity,' one of the most* treasured relics in the library of the Iliff School of Theology...." After a short recounting of the General Daniel Morgan version of the legend, Kuskulis concludes, the book... ...was presented ... to the Iliff School of Theology, where it now reposes in state, viewed thru the sanctity of its glass cabinet by hundreds of students and visitors annually. *"In spite of the age and wanderings of the book, it is remarkably well preserved. The skin is not broken or cracked; its smoothness and texture equal those of the finest parchment; its color has mellowed to deep ivory mottling into saffron, and by an ironic quirk of fate, it endures as a priceless vestment for the teachings of brotherly love."* (Emphasis added).[149]

Mid-1970s: Three White Iliff Students Concerned about Book

[By the mid-1970s with the Civil Rights movement,] the existence of this atrocity at Iliff became a concern to a small group of [white] Iliff students who found the triumphal public exhibit of the book in the Iliff library to be an "embarrassing and tragic fact," which led them to write a letter of appeal to the institution's president.[150]

While students protested the book's presence internally, they also made contact with the Denver Indian community through the Denver Indian Center and the Denver American Indian Movement chapter.[151]

Repatriation Proceedings

> Mr. Vincent Harvier (Quechan Nation), affiliated with both AIM and the Indian Center, returned the call and began the proceedings to repatriate the "human remains" of this Indian ancestor...[152]

The person who actually performed the task of separating the cover from the book was Iliff's assistant librarian, Jerry Campbell.[153] He used a blade to remove the cover, leaving the binding holding the book together intact. "I remember thinking, 'Good grief, this is the skin of a human being,'" he said. "This is a terrible thing to have here and be kind of celebrating it."[154]

On May 31, 1974, the Iliff board of trustees, voted as follows:

> ...to give the cover of the book to you [AIM], with the understanding that it would be properly buried according to Indian tradition, and with the request that no publicity of any kind be given. The Board acted out of respect for the Indian brother whose body was tragically mutilated many decades ago, and with genuine respect for the religious beliefs of Native American people.[155]

As stated by Emeritus Prof. George "Tink" Tinker, Ph.D.:

> At the time, Iliff leaders decided to maintain silence about the book and its cover, asking AIM and others with knowledge of the situation to sign a non-disclosure agreement "in order to protect Iliff in terms of its fundraising potential," Tinker said. "That's immoral and unethical," Tinker said of the secrecy. "... Christians have two words for it that we don't have in any Indian language. It was evil, and it was sinful."[156]

Book Cover Turned over to American Indian Movement

> "...a patch of human skin, stretched and tanned like an animal hide, was turned over to the American Indian Movement, hand-carried to Wyoming's Wind River Indian Reservation and quietly buried.

> ... No one knows where it is. ... The cover was given to Arapaho spiritual leaders ... Three-hundred-thirty miles to the southeast of that sacred burial ground sits a book without a cover locked in a safe in the basement of the Iliff School of Theology.¹⁵⁷

Confidentiality Broken by Prof. George "Tink" Tinker, an Osage Scholar Hired by Iliff in 1985

> ... the skin – and all the weight of history and violence absorbed in – would have stayed hidden had not a fellow professor told Prof. George "Tink" Tinker, an Osage scholar hired by Iliff in 1985, about the book, breaking that confidentiality. ... For a while, Tinker was so hurt he couldn't even speak about the book and considered quitting. ... I thanked the colleague for sharing this story, and as soon as possible I [privately] smoked out the entire school with cedar smoke (without being too intrusive—as a young upstart scholar on this faculty) and began to wonder whether I could even stay as a member of the faculty of the school.¹⁵⁸

Instead of leaving Iliff, in 2014, he wrote an exhaustively researched essay titled *"Red Skin, Tanned Hide: A Book of Christian History Bound in the Flayed Skin of an American Indian,"* which was published in the *Journal of Race, Ethnicity, and Religion.*¹⁵⁹

> Needless to say, American Indian people who know anything at all about this book, and especially Cheyenne and Arapaho people, often refuse to set foot on the Iliff campus, even if they know that the offensive cover is no longer wrapped around the book.¹⁶⁰

Iliff President Tom Wolfe Collaborates with Prof. Tinker on Course to Follow

> Enter newly appointed Iliff School of Theology President and CEO Rev. Thomas Wolfe, Ph.D., in 2013, who supported Tinker, nullified his nondisclosure obligations and vowed to take the issue head-on because, he told The Denver Gazette, "secrets kill people." [Rev. Wolfe had learned about the book in 1996 when he attended the General Conference of The United Methodist Church held in

Denver that year, a meeting of the highest legislative body of the Church. The General Conference is the body that sets official policy and speaks as the entire denomination. "A word was spreading across the Board at the General Conference because there was knowledge that there was some book at Iliff with the skin of a Native American person as its cover." When he became President, he was given a file marked Confidential, with information about the book.]¹⁶¹

"Just the idea of a book covered with the skin of a Native American person was profoundly disturbing," Wolfe told Rocky Mountain PBS. "You don't have to be affiliated with the school to feel that. It's part of a long history of violation of native peoples in this country." He said the book represents "not just one institution's lack of understanding but [also] the whole nature of Christian domination that misplaced and murdered millions of native people."¹⁶²

[Prof. Tinker and Pres. Wolfe became] intent on atoning for Iliff's dark past by leaving the decision of what to do with the coverless artifact in the hands of the Lenape people.¹⁶³

In April 2022, Wolfe and Tinker brought five Lenape (Delaware) representatives to Denver for a conference with school leaders to discuss the book.

In late April 2022 the following individuals met with Dr. Tom Wolfe and the Iliff Trustees: Curtis Zunigha (Delaware Tribe), Connie Fall Leaf (Delaware Tribe), Pat Noah (Eelunaapeewi Lahkeewiit – Delaware, Canada), Gregory Miller (Stockbridge-Munsee), plus Wes Martel (Shoshone/Arapaho), Steve Newcomb (Shawnee/Lenape) and Robert Cross (Lakota).¹⁶⁴

Mr. Zunigha stated: "We recognize this as a teachable moment." ... Mr. Zunigha said that the spiritual force of the murdered Lenape man whose skin covered Iliff's book remains centuries after his death. ... Another elder at the meetings was Patricia Noah, who said she reacted with "disgust and sadness and heartache" when Zunigha told her about the Iliff book. "I think that [murdered] man's spirit got caught between this physical world and the spiritual world," she said. "He couldn't get to the spiritual world because part of him was put on that book. Part of his spirit stayed there and was stuck there."[165]

To the Delaware:

> The literal separation of skin from one of the Lenape victims, all in the service of glorifying the history of Christianity, was emblematic of all the separations that Native peoples experienced during domination and conquest, colonization, extermination, removal, and assimilation at the hands of Eurochristian invaders.
>
> The questions that long survived this incident were 1) why maintain the secrecy of Iliff's reprehensible behavior, and 2) what should be done with the remainder of the book? Early in his tenure as president, President Wolfe decided that the narrative of the book's history should become a teaching moment for both Iliff and the rest of the world. What Iliff once displayed with perverse pride, and then hid away with equally abject shame, Iliff now intends to use transparently as a teaching tool and as an occasion for reshaping its whole theological presence in the world. And they intend it as a moment for building right relationships with American Indian Peoples, particularly with the Lenape.

The Delaware Indian News proclaimed the following course of action sought by the Lenape Elders: A Statement of Guidance and Direction:

> As the Delegation of Lenape Elders, we are calling on the Iliff School of Theology to develop funds and resources to accomplish the following:
> • Commit to maintaining a permanent relationship with Lenape Elders
> • Create an Endowed Professorship with a Job Description by Lenape Elders. The expectation is that the professorship would always be filled by an American Indian activist scholar
> • Add a required curriculum course to educate all Iliff theology students in a clear understanding of the Papal Bulls and the Doctrine of Discovery and Domination
> • Create a Memorial and/or Traveling Display, also available on the Internet, featuring passages of the book with audio recordings read by Iliff theology students
> • An Interpretive Center to educate Indians and non-Indians [on] the

truths of American history as it pertains to the Indigenous nations and people of Turtle Island
• At such time as it is requested by the Lenape, the Elders will take possession of the book.¹⁶⁶

Interpretive Center at Iliff

It was noted in the PBS documentary:

> "A memorial tells his story, an interpretive center tells our story," Zunigha said.
>
> A team at Iliff has started work on the interpretive center, which is centered around education. It will be a space where Indians and non-Indians can learn about the book's history and how it applies to the wider history of Euro-Christian domination in America. The Iliff team identified a space in the library for the center and took suggestions from the Lenape delegation during their April 18 visit.
>
> [One of the Lenape Elders] Falleaf expressed appreciation for the work Iliff had done but was disappointed by the size of the space for the interpretive center.
>
> "The Lenape room needs to be comfortable for our people and for other people like us to pray and to learn and to think about our own histories, family histories, the national histories of each of our people. We need space for that," Falleaf explained.¹⁶⁷

Iliff Agreed to Relationship with Lenape People

President Wolfe used these words about establishing a relationship with the Lenape people:

> I too [like the Trustees] think it would be an honor, but Iliff has already been in a destructive relationship with the Lenape people because of the book. We can't use the word 'reconciliation' because there's been no conciliation. I recommend something new, but something with the entire past in mind. I recommend a new and renewed relationship with Lenape people.

For now, the book will stay at Iliff. Said Zunigha: "The sense of response and commitment from Iliff will ... inform and frame our attitude about taking possession of this book and making things right by that ancestor."[168]

"Changing a worldview ... happens over a lifetime, but it doesn't happen until people start thinking a different way," Tinker said. "That's what I want, for Iliff and for all of my Euro-Christian relatives."[169]

Statement of Iliff School of Theology

The Board of Trustees and the leadership of Iliff School of Theology commit to a permanent relationship with the Lenape elders and their successors toward building a new history and relationship in full recognition of Iliff's history of possession of the book of Christian history covered in the skin of a Lenape man.

Until such time when the Lenape leaders take possession of the book, it will remain in a secure and respectful place within the President's office. The tobacco that was placed at the center of the initial meeting with the elders will continue to rest upon it.[170]

President Wolfe's Goal regarding Iliff's Commitment to Lenape People Going Forward

One of the things that I thought was really important for us to do was to talk about building this into the institution so that it will not be dependent on any one personality or any one person's particular belief that this is a good thing to do but rather this is going to be a commitment that this generation is making for this institution going forward in time. One hundred years from now what is Iliff going to be doing and how is it going to be understanding this situation and what is it going to be teaching about Christian dominance against Native American people?[171]

As stated in the Delaware Indian News:

For some decades many Indian people would refuse to enter Iliff because of this egregious book and its history. But that history is part and parcel of the history of this country. Now Iliff is proactively committed to changing that historical memory. And as we have said consistently, healing for Iliff is a process in which all of us help to ensure that Iliff will never forget its role in this gruesome history. We call on the whole of the Iliff constituency to stand with Iliff in this historic endeavor. This will necessarily command our intention for years to come.[172]

Rev. Wolfe, 2023 IAMSCU Flame of Excellence Award for His Contribution While President at Iliff (2013-2023)

On December 11, 2023, the International Association of Methodist Schools, Colleges, and Universities (IAMSCU) made the following announcement:

> Tonight in Atlanta, GA, IAMSCU had a special celebration highlighting the presentation to Dr. Thomas V. Wolfe of The Ken Yamada Distinguished Leadership Award, "The Flame of Excellence". This is the highest award given by IAMSCU, *in recognition of his outstanding presidency* and his history-making contributions to Methodist education worldwide.
> *The subject of the conference in Atlanta, "Human Rights and the Indigenous Peoples of North America", has been of special interest to Dr. Wolfe, having addressed it courageously and forthrightly during his presidency at Iliff School of Theology and initiated the reflection on this subject within IAMSCU.*
> Dr. Tink Tinker introduced Dr. Wolfe. Dr. Ken Yamada personally presented the award, and Dr. Gerald L. Durley – who participated in the Civil Rights Movement with Dr. Martin Luther King Jr. and served as adviser to Dr. Wolfe at Iliff give a speech honoring him. Congratulations Dr. Wolfe! (Emphasis added).[173]

APPENDIX 1

COUNTY	COUNTY SEAT	TRIBES
ADAMS	AURORA, ARVADA, COMMERCE CITY	ARAPAHO ("ARAP") & CHEYENNE ("CHEY")
ALAMOSA	SAN LUIS, SAND DUNES	CAPOTE & MOUACHE UTES
ARAPAHOE	LITTLETON AURORA ENGLEWOOD	ARAP/CHEY (1867 MEDICINE LODGE TREATY - OK IND. TERR. RES.)
ARCHULETA	PAGOSA SPRINGS	UTES
BACA	SPRINGFIELD, COMANCHE NATIONAL GRASSLANDS	COMANCHES
BENT	LAS ANIMAS	CHEYENNE, COMANCHES, KIOWAS
BOULDER	BOULDER	ARAP/CHEY
BROOMFIELD	BROOMFIELD	ARAP/CHEY
CHAFFEE	SALIDA	
CHEYENNE	CHEYENNE WELLS	ARAP/CHEY
CLEAR CREEK	IDAHO SPRINGS, LOVELAND, GEORGETOWN	ARAP/CHEY (UTES)
CONEJOS	ANTONITO	UTES - CAPOTES
COSTILLA	SAN LUIS	UTES - FT. GARLAND
CROWLEY	ORDWAY	ARAP/CHEY (KIOWAS, JICARILLA APACHES, COMANCHES)
CUSTER	WESTCLIFFE - SOUTH CENTRAL CO	UTES

DELTA	DELTA	PARIANUCHE UTES TABEGUACHE UTES
DENVER	DENVER	ARAP/CHEY
DOLORES	DOVE CREEK	WEEMINUCHE UTES
DOUGLAS	CASTLEROCK, LONE TREE PARKER	ARAP/CHEY (UTES)
EAGLE	EAGLE, VAIL, WHITE RIVER NAT'L FOREST	PARIANUCHE, YAMPA UTES
EL PASO	PIKES PEAK	TABEGUACHE UTES
ELBERT	ELIZABETH	ARAP/CHEY (COMANCHE, KIOWA, UTES)
FREMONT	ROYAL GORGE, CANON CITY	MUACHE UTES (CHEYENNE, ARAP, KIOWA, COMANCHES)
GARFIELD	GLENWOOD SPRINGS	PARIANUCHE UTES
GILPIN	CENTRAL CITY	UINTAH & YAMPA UTES (ARAP)
GRAND	GRANBY (WINTER PARK)	UINTAH UTES (MIDDLE PARK INDIAN AGENCY) ARAP
GUNNISON	CRESTED BUTTE	PARIANUCHE UTES, TABEGUACHE UTES
HINSDALE	SILVERTON, SAN JUAN MT.	WEEMINUCHE, CAPOTE, TABEGUACHE UTES (BRUNOT AG.)
HUERFANO	WALSENBERG	UTES FOUGHT JICARILLA APACHE & COMANCHE
JACKSON	NORTH PARK, WALDEN	YAMPARIKA UTES 1865, 1869 UTES DROVE PROSPECTORS OUT

JEFFERSON	ARVADA, LAKEWOOD, RED ROCKS, ROCKY FLATS	ARAP/CHEY (UTES)
KIOWA	EADS, SAND CREEK MASS., SUMMIT SPRINGS	KIOWA, COMANCHE, ARAP, CHEY
KIT CARSON	BURLINGTON	ARAP, CHEY
LA PLATA	DURANGO, FT. LEWIS	WEEMINUCHE (IGNACIO), CAPOTE, MUACHE (BUCKSKIN CHARLIE - SAPIAH)
LAKE	LEADVILLE	PARIANUCHE UTES
LARIMER	FORT COLLINS	UTES, ARAP, CHEY
LAS ANIMAS	TRINIDAD	MOACHE UTES (JIC. APACHE, COMANCHE)
LINCOLN	HUGO (LIMON)	ARAP/CHEY/KIOWA EARLY 1800'S PAWNEE/ APACHE ALLIANCE
LOGAN	STERLING	ARAP/CHEY/KIOWA
MESA	GRAND JUNCTION	UTES (REMOVED FROM GUNNISON, COLORADO, & UNCOMPAHGRE RIVER VALLEYS)
MINERAL	CREEDE	WEEMINUCHE, CAPOTE UTES
MOFFAT	CRAIG, FT. MORGAN	YAMPA, UINTAH, PARIANUCHE UTES (ARAP/CHEY/KIOWA)
MONTEZUMA	CORTEZ, MESA VERDE	UTES
MONTROSE	MONTROSE	PARIANUCHE, TABEGUACHE, & WEEMINUCHE UTES

MORGAN	FORT MORGAN	ARAP/CHEY
OTERO	LA JUNTA	CHEYENNE, ARAP, COMANCHE
OURAY	OURAY	UTES
PARK	FAIRPLAY, PIKE NAT'L FOREST, SOUTH PARK	TABEGUACHE UTES 1859 KILLED PROSPECTORS (ARAP/CHEY/KIOWA/COMANCHE)
PHILLIPS	HOLYOKE	(ARAP/CHEY/KIOWA/ COMANCHE/ PAWNEE/ LAKOTA)
PITKIN	ASPEN	PARIANUCHE UTES
PROWERS	LAMAR	COMANCHE MASSIVE HORSE HERDS (KIOWA, CHEYENNE)
PUEBLO	PUEBLO	TABEGUACHE, MUACHE UTES, CHEYENNE
RIO BLANCO	MEEKER	PARIANUCHE, YAMPA, UINTAH UTES
RIO GRANDE	MONTE VISTA	UTES (CHEYENNE, COMANCHE, APACHE, & NAVAJO)
ROUTT	STEAMBOAT	YAMPA UTES
SAGUACHE	SAGUACHE	TABEGUACHE, MUACHE & CAPOTE UTES, NAVAJO, COMANCHE, CHEY, ARAP & KIOWA)
SAN JUAN	SILVERTON	TABEGUACHE & WEEMINUCHE UTES
SAN MIGUEL	TELLURIDE	WEEMINUCHE UTES

Roberta Carol Harvey

SEDGWICK	JULESBURG	ARAP/CHEY (CAMP RANKIN PROTECT STAGE LINES & EMIGRANTS)
SUMMIT	BRECKENRIDGE	UTE & ARAPAHO CONFLICT OVER AREA
TELLER	CRIPPLE CREEK	TABEGUACHE UTES
WASHINGTON	AKRON	CHEY/ARAP
WELD	GREELEY	CHEY/ARAP
YUMA	WRAY	CHEY/ARAP

Notes: Colorado

1. Warren L. d'Azevedo, et al. (eds.), (The Current Status of Anthropological Research in the Great Basin; 1964.) Reno: Desert Research Institute, 1966, p. 178. See also: James Grady, Environmental Factors in Archaeological Site Location, Piceance Basin, Colorado. (Denver: Bureau of Land Management, 1980). Athearn, Frederic J. An Isolated Empire: A History of Northwestern Colorado. 3rd ed. Colorado Bureau of Land Management, Cultural Resource Series No. 2, 1982, p. 3. https://upload.wikimedia.org/wikipedia/commons/8/86/The_new_empire_of_the_Rockies_-_a_history_of_northeast_Colorado_%28IA_newempireofrocki00mehl%29.pdf (accessed online Dec. 7, 2022).
2. American Blood on American Soil, U.S. History. https://www.ushistory.org/us/29c.asp (accessed online November 11, 2020).
3. Around the world with General Grant: a narrative of the visit of General U.S. Grant, ex-President of the United States, to various countries in Europe, Asia, and Africa, in 1877, 1878, 1879 to which are added certain conversations with General Grant on questions connected with American politics and history, John Russell Young, 1879: 448.
4. Address by General John Pope before the Social Science Association, at Cincinnati, Ohio, May 24, 1878. Delivered by Request of the Association (Cincinnati: n.p., 1878).
5. 1904 - Indian Affairs - Laws and Treaties, Treaties Vol. II, Charles J.

Kappler (2019). U.S. and Indian Relations. 594.
6. Report of the Commissioner of Indian Affairs to the Secretary of the Interior, United States. Office of Indian Affairs. 1853, p. 128.
7. King, Judy. "Upper Arkansas Indian Agency." Colorado Encyclopedia. https://coloradoencyclopedia.org/article/upper-arkansas-indian-agency (accessed online Dec. 23, 2021).
8. ALICE POLK HILL, COLORADO PIONEERS IN PICTURE AND STORY, 1915. https://archive.org/details/coloradopioneers00hill_0 (accessed online Dec. 23, 2021).
9. Report of the Commissioner of Indian Affairs to the Secretary of the Interior, United States. Office of Indian Affairs. 1859, p. 21.
10. Ibid., p. 129.
11. Id.
12. Id.
13. Ibid., pp. 130-131.
14. Ibid., p. 137.
15. Ibid., p. 138.
16. Report of the Commissioner of Indian Affairs to the Secretary of the Interior, United States. Office of Indian Affairs. 1859, pp. 138-139.
17. Report of the Commissioner of Indian Affairs to the Secretary of the Interior, United States. Office of Indian Affairs. 1859, p. 20.
18. Stephen Arnold Douglas, Speeches of Senator S. A. Douglas: On the Occasion of His Public Receptions by the Citizens of New Orleans, Philadelphia, and Baltimore, L. Towers, 1859, Harvard University.
19. Reminiscences of Lincoln, Address by General O.O. Howard to Young Men's Republican Club, Montpelier, Vt., Feb. 12, 1896. https://library.bowdoin.edu/arch/mss/ooh-pdf/M91b40f039.pdf (accessed online March 12, 2023). S. Exec. Doc. No. 15, 36th Cong., 1st Sess. (1860).
20. Hall, Frank. History of the State of Colorado, Embracing Accounts of the Pre-historic Races and Their Remains: The Earliest Spanish, French and American Explorations... the First American Settlements Founded; the Original Discoveries of Gold in the Rocky Mountains; the Development of Cities and Towns, with the Various Phases of Industrial and Political Transition, from 1858 to 1890..., Vol. 4, Blakely Printing Company, 1895.
21. Report of the Commissioner of Indian Affairs to the Secretary of the Interior, United States. Office of Indian Affairs. 1861, p. 17.
22. Cuthair v. Montezuma-Cortez Colo. Sch. Dist. No. Re-1, 7 F. Supp.

2d 1152, 1156 (D. Colo. 1998).

23. Report of the Commissioner of Indian Affairs to the Secretary of the Interior, United States. Office of Indian Affairs. 1862, p. 13.

24. https://www.whitehousehistory.org/photographs-of-indian-delegates-in-the-presidents-summer-house (accessed online Feb. 3, 2023).

25. https://www.whitehousehistory.org/photographs-of-indian-delegates-in-the-presidents-summer-house (accessed online Feb. 3, 2023).

26. Letter of William P. Dole to John Evans, 07-16-1863, Governor's Papers, Transcript of original Letter Press Book Record. Governor John Evans. Colorado State Archives, History Colorado. MSS Evans 226.

27. Report of the John Evans Study Committee, University of Denver, Nov. 2014, Denver, p. 45.

28. Report of the Commissioner of Indian Affairs to the Secretary of the Interior, United States. Office of Indian Affairs. 1863, p. 28.

29. Ibid., p. 139.

30. Encyclopedia Staff. "Conejos Treaty." Colorado Encyclopedia. https://coloradoencyclopedia.org/article/conejos-treaty (accessed online Feb. 3, 2023).

31. The War of the Rebellion: A Compilation of the Official Records of the Union and Confederate Armies, United States War Department, 1891. Series I, Vol. XLI, Part IV, Chapter XLVI, CORRESPONDENCE, ETC. - UNION, p. 101.

32. A Timeline of events relating to the Sand Creek Massacre. National Park Service. https://www.nps.gov/sand/learn/timeline.htm (accessed online Feb. 19, 2023).

33. Draper, Kenneth E. The Pike's Peakers and the Rocky Mountain Rangers: A History of Colorado in the Civil War. Xlibris Corporation, 2012, p. 320.

34. The War of the Rebellion: A Compilation of the Official Records of the Union and Confederate Armies, United States War Department, 1891. LOUISIANA AND THE TRANS-MISSISSIPPI. Chapter XLVI, SKIRMISH NEAR FREMONT'S ORCHARD, COLO., p. 883.

35. Report of the University of Denver John Evans Study Committee, p. 55.

36. The War of the Rebellion: A Compilation of the Official Records of the Union and Confederate Armies, United States War Department, 1891. Series I, Vol. XXXIV, Part I, Chapter XLVI, LOUISIANA AND THE TRANS-MISSISSIPPI, SKIRMISH AT CEDAR BLUFFS,

Colorado., pp. 909-910.

37. The War of the Rebellion: A Compilation of the Official Records of the Union and Confederate Armies, United States War Department, 1891. Series I, Vol. XXXIV, Part IV, CORRESPONDENCE, ETC. - UNION, p. 151.

38. John M. Chivington. http://www.shoppbs.pbs.org/weta/thewest/people/a_c/chivington.htm (accessed online Feb. 19, 2023).

39. https://www.nps.gov/sand/learn/news/hungate-family-murdered.htm (accessed online Dec. 27, 2021).

40. Mehls, Steven F. The new empire of the Rockies: A history of northeast Colorado. No. 16. Bureau of Land Management, 1984, p. 43. https://upload.wikimedia.org/wikipedia/commons/8/86/The_new_empire_of_the_Rockies_-_a_history_of_northeast_Colorado_%28IA_newempireofrocki00mehl%29.pdf (accessed online Dec. 7, 2022).

41. Kathy Alexander. https://www.legendsofamerica.com/fort-collins/ (accessed online Oct. 5, 2022).

42. Mehls, Steven F. The new empire of the Rockies: A history of northeast Colorado. No. 16. Bureau of Land Management, 1984, p. 43.

43. The War of the Rebellion: A Compilation of the Official Records of the Union and Confederate Armies, United States War Department, 1891. Series I, Vol. XXXIV, Part IV, CORRESPONDENCE, ETC. - UNION, p. 206.

44. The War of the Rebellion: A Compilation of the Official Records of the Union and Confederate Armies, United States War Department, 1891. Series I, Vol. XXXIV, Part IV, CORRESPONDENCE, ETC. - UNION, p. 320.

45. Ibid., p. 353.

46. Ibid., p. 381.

47. Ibid., pp. 402-404.

48. Ibid., pp. 421-422.

49. Report of the Commissioner of Indian Affairs to the Secretary of the Interior, United States. Office of Indian Affairs. Colorado Superintendency. 1864, pp. 218-219.

50. The War of the Rebellion: A Compilation of the Official Records of the Union and Confederate Armies, United States War Department, 1891. Series I, Vol. XXXIV, Part IV, CORRESPONDENCE, ETC. - UNION, p. 658.

51. Id.

52. Report of the Commissioner of Indian Affairs to the Secretary of the Interior, United States. Office of Indian Affairs. Colorado Superintendency. 1864, pp. 230-231.
53. Report of the John Evans Study Committee, University of Denver, Nov. 2014, Denver, pp. 63, 64, 65, 66, 69.
54. The War of the Rebellion: A Compilation of the Official Records of the Union and Confederate Armies, United States War Department, 1891. Series I, Vol. XXXIV, Part IV, Chapter LIII, CORRESPONDENCE, ETC. - UNION, p. 695.
55. Ibid., p. 765.
56. Ibid., p. 775.
57. A Timeline of events relating to the Sand Creek Massacre. https://www.nps.gov/sand/learn/timeline.htm (accessed online Sep. 25, 2021).
58. The War of the Rebellion: A Compilation of the Official Records of the Union and Confederate Armies, United States War Department, 1891. Series I, Vol. XLI, Part III, Chapter LIII, CORRESPONDENCE, ETC. - UNION, pp. 195-196.
59. Ibid., p. 195.
60. Ibid., p. 242.
61. Condition of the Indian Tribes: Report of the Joint Special Committee, Appointed Under Joint Resolution of March 3, 1865, United States, Congress. Joint Special Committee to Inquire into Condition of the Indian Tribes, Kraus Reprint Company, p. 87.
62. The Sand Creek Massacre Weld Council Transcript. https://www.kclonewolf.com/History/SandCreek/sc-documents/sc-weld-council.html (accessed online Oct. 2, 2021).
63. Report of the John Evans Study Committee, University of Denver, Nov. 2014, Denver, pp. 13, 73.
64. The War of the Rebellion: A Compilation of the Official Records of the Union and Confederate Armies, United States War Department, 1891. Series I, Vol. XLI, Part III, Chapter LIII, CORRESPONDENCE, ETC. - UNION, pp. 494-495.
65. The War of the Rebellion: A Compilation of the Official Records of the Union and Confederate Armies, United States War Department, 1891. Series I, Vol. XLI, Part III, Chapter LIII, CORRESPONDENCE, ETC. - UNION, p. 495.
66. Ibid., p. 525.
67. Ibid., p. 876.

68. Report of the Commissioner of Indian Affairs to the Secretary of the Interior, United States. Office of Indian Affairs. 1864, p. 256.
69. The War of the Rebellion: A Compilation of the Official Records of the Union and Confederate Armies, United States War Department, 1891. Series I, Vol. XLI, Part IV, Chapter LIII, CORRESPONDENCE, ETC. - UNION, p. 433.
70. Ibid., p. 876.
71. Report of the Commissioner of Indian Affairs to the Secretary of the Interior, United States. Office of Indian Affairs. 1864, p. 23.
72. The War of the Rebellion: A Compilation of the Official Records of the Union and Confederate Armies, United States War Department, 1891. Series I, Vol. XLI, Part III, Chapter LIII, CORRESPONDENCE, ETC. - UNION, p. 914.
73. Ibid., p. 708.
74. Ibid., p. 709.
75. The War of the Rebellion: A Compilation of the Official Records of the Union and Confederate Armies, United States War Department, 1891. Series I, Vol. XLI, Part I, LOUISIANA AND THE TRANS-MISSISSIPPI, Chapter LIII, p. 948.
76. Report of the Commissioner of Indian Affairs to the Secretary of the Interior, United States. Office of Indian Affairs. Central Superintendency. 1865, p. 387.
77. Report of the Commissioner of Indian Affairs to the Secretary of the Interior, United States. Office of Indian Affairs. 1865, p. 24.
78. AW Bowen & Co. Progressive Men of Western Colorado... AW Bowen & Company, 1905, pp. 627-628. https://babel.hathitrust.org/cgi/pt?id=uc2.ark:/13960/t9n29vf9s&view=1up&seq=668&q1=Sand%20creek (accessed online Dec. 7, 2022).
79. The War of the Rebellion: A Compilation of the Official Records of the Union and Confederate Armies, United States War Department, 1891. Series I, Vol. XLI, Part IV, LOUISIANA AND THE TRANS-MISSISSIPPI, Chapter LIII, CORRESPONDENCE, ETC.- UNION, p. 797.
80. Ibid., pp. 953-954.
81. Report of the John Evans Study Committee, University of Denver, Nov. 2014, Denver, p. iii.
82. The War of the Rebellion: A Compilation of the Official Records of the Union and Confederate Armies, Chapter LIII. ENGAGEMENT ON

SAND CREEK, COLO. TER., United States War Department, 1891. Series I, Vol. XLI, Part IV, CORRESPONDENCE, ETC. - UNION, pp. 970-971.
83. Patrick J. Jung, The Black Hawk War of 1832 (Norman: University of Oklahoma Press, 2007), 33-210.
84. Report of the Commissioner of Indian Affairs to the Secretary of the Interior, United States. Office of Indian Affairs. 1865, p. 431.
85. Ibid., p. 400.
86. Ibid., p. 525.
87. Ibid., p. 523.
88. Ibid., p. 527.
89. Encyclopedia Staff. "Little Arkansas Treaty." Colorado Encyclopedia. https://coloradoencyclopedia.org/article/little-arkansas-treaty (accessed online Feb. 3, 2023).
90. https://thejulesburgproject.org/ (accessed online Feb. 4, 2023).
91. Browne, John Ross, and James Wickes Taylor. Reports upon the mineral resources of the United States. 1867. Report of James W. Taylor, special commissioner for the collection of statistics upon gold and silver mining east of the Rocky mountains. Feb. 15, 1867. 39th Congress, 2d Session. House of Representatives. Ex. Doc. No. 92.
92. Report of the Commissioner of Indian Affairs to the Secretary of the Interior, United States. Office of Indian Affairs, Central Superintendency. 1866, pp. 158-160.
93. Report of the Commissioner of Indian Affairs to the Secretary of the Interior, Accompanying Papers. REPORT TO THE PRESIDENT BY THE INDIAN PEACE COMMISSION, JANUARY 7, 1868. United States. Office of Indian Affairs. 1868, p. 38.
94. The Burlington Weekly Sentinel, June 28, 1867; The Chicago Evening Post, June 26, 1867.
95. Athearn, Frederic J. Land of Contrast: A History of Southeast Colorado. Colorado Bureau of Land Management, Cultural Resource Series No. 17, 1985, p. 79.
96. Report of the Commissioner of Indian Affairs to the Secretary of the Interior, United States. Office of Indian Affairs. 1870, p. 163.
97. Kathy Alexander. https://www.legendsofamerica.com/battle-summit-springs-colorado/ (accessed online Feb. 4, 2023).
98. https://www.ghosttowns.com/states/co/summitspringsbattlefield.html (accessed online Feb. 4, 2023).

99. The Battle of Summit Springs, Clarence Reckmeyer, The Colorado Magazine, The State Historical Society of Colorado, Vol. VI, No. 6, Nov. 1929.

100. https://www.ksgenweb.org/archives/statewide/history/roenigk/chpt32.htm (accessed online Feb. 4, 2023).

101. Hall, Frank, pp. 191-192.

102. Report of the Commissioner of Indian Affairs to the Secretary of the Interior, United States. Office of Indian Affairs. 1873, p. 258.

103. Hall, Frank, pp. 60-61.

104. Report of the Commissioner of Indian Affairs to the Secretary of the Interior, United States. Office of Indian Affairs. 1877, p. 45.

105. Report of the Commissioner of Indian Affairs to the Secretary of the Interior, United States. Office of Indian Affairs. 1877, p. 6.

106. The American Military on the Frontier: The Proceedings of the 7th Military History Symposium, United States Air Force Academy, 30 September-1 October 1976, Ed. James P. Tate, Office of Air Force History, Headquarters USAF, 1978.

107. Dee Brown, Bury My Heart at Wounded Knee (New York: Henry Holt and Co., 1970), 367.

108. U.S. Congress, House, Extinguishment of Indian Title, 46th Cong., 1st sess., Congressional Record, vol. 9, pt. 1, 21 April 1870, 615.

109. Carl, Ubbelohde, Maxine Benson, and Duane A. Smith, A Colorado History (Boulder, Colorado: Pruett Publishing, 1988), 190.

110. https://upload.wikimedia.org/wikipedia/commons/8/86/The_new_empire_of_the_Rockies_-_a_history_of_northeast_Colorado_%28IA_newempireofrocki00mehl%29.pdf (accessed online Dec. 7, 2022).

111. U.S. Congress, House, The Committee on Indian Affairs, Testimony in Relation to the Ute Indian Outbreak, p. 10.

112. Parkhill, Forbes. The Wildest of the West. "The Meeker Massacre." Denver: Sage, 1957, p. 235.

113. Brown, Dee. Bury My Heart at Wounded Knee.

114. Elmer R. Burkey, "The Thornburgh Battle With the Utes on Milk River," The Colorado Magazine 13 (May 1936): 93.

115. War Department, General of the Army, Annual Report of the Secretary of War (1880).

116. Hall, Frank, p. 500.

117. Athearn, Frederic J. An Isolated Empire: A History of Northwestern Colorado. 3rd ed. Colorado Bureau of Land Management, Cultural

Resource Series No. 2, 1982, p. 53.
118. U.S. Congress, House, Extinguishment of Indian Title, 46th Cong., 1st sess., Congressional Record, vol. 9, pt. l, 21 April 1880, 615.
119. Report of the Commissioner of Indian Affairs to the Secretary of the Interior, United States. Office of Indian Affairs. 1879, pp. xxi-xxii.
120. Athearn, Frederic J. An Isolated Empire: A History of Northwestern Colorado. 3rd ed. Colorado Bureau of Land Management, Cultural Resource Series No. 2, 1982, p. 49.
121. Hall, Frank, pp. 494-495.
122. United States Congress. House. The Committee on Indian Affairs. Testimony in Relation to the Ute Indian Outbreak. Hearings 46th Cong., 2d Session. House Misc. Doc. 33, March 1880.
123. Testimony in Relation to Ute Outbreak, 46th Congress, 2nd Session, House Miscellaneous Documents no. 38, 1880, p. 101.
124. Ibid., p. 2.
125. LeRoy R. Hafen, "Otto Mears, 'Pathfinder of the San Juan'," The Colorado Magazine, 9 (March 1932): 73.
126. The Ute Campaign of 1879: A Study in the Use of the Military Instrument, Russel Dale Santala, U.S. Army Command and General Staff College, 1994, University of Georgia Libraries, p. 70. Citing Thomas C. Leonard, Above the Battle: War-Making in America from Appomattox to Versailles (New York: Oxford University Press, 1978), p. 46.
127. Denver Daily Times, Sep. 12, 1881.
128. Athearn, Frederic J. An Isolated Empire: A History of Northwestern Colorado. 3rd ed. Colorado Bureau of Land Management, Cultural Resource Series No. 2, 1982, p. 4.
129. House Journal of the Legislative Assembly of the Territory of Colorado, Colorado. Legislative Assembly. House of Representatives, 1881, pp. 321, 388, 409, 455, 756.
130. Report of the Commissioner of Indian Affairs to the Secretary of the Interior, United States. Office of Indian Affairs. 1890, p. XLIV. Letter from the Secretary of the Interior, transmitting a communication from Attorney-General and report of Commissioner of General Land Office, also report of Commissioner of Indian Affairs, in response to Senate resolution of January 10, 1882, calling for information touching the opening for settlement under the pre-emption laws of the United States of part of the Ute Reservation in Colorado. 130 S. Exec. Doc. No. 108, 47th Cong., 1st Sess. (1882).

131. Letter from the Secretary of the Interior, transmitting, in response to Senate resolutions of January 27, 1881, copy of report of Ute Commission, and copies of all correspondence between this department and the Ute Commission, and also the Governor of Colorado, concerning the same since June 15, 1880. S. Exec. Doc. No. 31, 46th Cong., 3rd Sess. (1881).

132. Edmund B. Rogers, "Notes on the Establishment of Mesa Verde National Park, The Colorado Magazine. XXIX, 1 (January 1952).

133. https://www.nps.gov/articles/lee-story-creating.htm (accessed online October 1, 2022).

134. Mesa Verde National Park, House Rep. No. 4944, 59th Cong., 1st Sess. (1906), pp. 1-2.

135. Congressional Record. 59th Congress, 1st Session, 1906, XL, Part 9, p. 8818.

136. Secretary of the Interior to Commissioner of the General Land Office, May 25, 1911, NA-RG 79. Assistant Secretary to Acting Superintendent Wright, Mesa Verde, July 25, 1911, NA-RG 79. 7. Superintendent, Annual Report, 1910; Acting Superintendent Wright to the Secretary, June 29, 1911, NA-RG 79.

137. Philip F. Anschutz with William J. Convery and Thomas J. Noel, Out Where the West Begins: Profiles, Visions and Strategies of Early Western Business Leaders (Denver: Cloud Camp Press, 2015), p. 236.

138. Flowers, Kaylyn Mercuri. "William N. Byers." Colorado Encyclopedia. https://coloradoencyclopedia.org/article/william-n-byers (accessed online Dec. 15, 2022).

139. MINING IN COLORADO A HISTORY OF DISCOVERY, DEVELOPMENT AND PRODUCTION BY CHARLES W. HENDERSON, DEPARTMENT OF THE INTERIOR, Hubert Work, Secretary U.S. GEOLOGICAL SURVEY, George Otis Smith, Director, Professional Paper 138, Washington Government Printing Office, 1926, p. 249.

140. Koschmann, A. H., and M. H. Bergendahl. "Principal Gold-Producing Districts." United States Geological Survey, Professional Paper 610, 1968.

141. https://coloradogeologicalsurvey.org/minerals/ (accessed online Dec. 28, 2021); Western Mining History. https://westernmininghistory.com/2099/the-top-ten-gold-producing-states/ (accessed online Jan. 31, 2023); Annual Report of the Department of the Interior, Volume 3,

1890, p. 645.

142. Mining and Engineering World, Volume 22, 1905, pp. 604-605; Aspen Evening Chronicle (Oct. 5, 1892).

143. https://denvergazette.com/premium/decades-after-displaying-book-bound-with-human-skin-denver-s-iliff-school-of-theology-still/article_29e32eae-4113-11ed-8482-9fbbaf77d202.html (accessed online February 2, 2024).

144. https://delawaretown.missouristate.edu/removal.html (accessed online July 8, 2023).

145. Lënapeí Pampil (Delaware Indian News) Building Right Relationships With American Indian Peoples Tink Tinker and Loring Abeyta, Denver Colorado, July 2022 PREFACE by Curtis Zunigha (enrolled member of Delaware Tribe, Bartlesville, OK), p. 6. https://delawaretribe.org/wp-content/uploads/din-2023-01.pdf (accessed online February 2, 2024).

146. Colorado Voices: A New Chapter, Oct. 20, 2022. Rocky Mountain Public Television. https://www.rmpbs.org/blogs/news/iliff-school-of-theology-lenape-nation-book/ (accessed online February 2, 2024).

147. Samuel Western, The Wyoming Cattle Boom, 1868-1886, 2014, A Project of the Wyoming Historical Society.

148. Athearn, Frederic J. An Isolated Empire: A History of Northwestern Colorado. 3rd ed. Colorado Bureau of Land Management, Cultural Resource Series No. 2, 1982, p. 4.

149. Kuskulis, "Iliff Library Has Old Book Bound in Slain Indian's Skin," Rocky Mountain News (February 12, 1934).

150. Letter to President Jameson Jones, May 30, 1974, from students Dave Randle, Mike Hartman, and Mike Hickcox. "Request of the American Indian Movement Concerning a book bound in the skin of an American Indian," p. 2. Iliff Library archives. Tinker, Tink. "Redskin, Tanned Hide: A Book of Christian History Bound in the Flayed Skin of an American Indian." *Journal of Race, Ethnicity, and Religion* 5.9 (2014): p. 32.

151. Tinker, Tink. "Redskin, Tanned Hide: A Book of Christian History Bound in the Flayed Skin of an American Indian." *Journal of Race, Ethnicity, and Religion* 5.9 (2014): p. 32.

152. Ibid., pp. 32- 33.

153. Ibid., p. 10.

154. Iliff School of Theology reckons with grisly past. https://www.christiancentury.org/article/news/iliff-school-theology-reckons-grisly-past (accessed online February 2, 2024).

155. Letter from President Jones (having been amended and vetted by Iliff attorney Victor Quinn) to Vincent Harvier, July 1, 1974. Iliff library archives. Tinker, Tink. "Redskin, Tanned Hide: A Book of Christian History Bound in the Flayed Skin of an American Indian." *Journal of Race, Ethnicity, and Religion* 5.9 (2014): pp. 35-36.

156. Colorado Voices: A New Chapter, Oct. 20, 2022. Rocky Mountain Public Television. https://www.rmpbs.org/blogs/news/iliff-school-of-theology-lenape-nation-book/ (accessed online February 2, 2024).

157. https://denvergazette.com/premium/decades-after-displaying-book-bound-with-human-skin-denver-s-iliff-school-of-theology-still/article_29e32eae-4113-11ed-8482-9fbbaf77d202.html (accessed online February 2, 2024).

158. Tinker, Tink. "Redskin, Tanned Hide: A Book of Christian History Bound in the Flayed Skin of an American Indian." *Journal of Race, Ethnicity, and Religion* 5.9 (2014): p. 10.

159. Ibid., p. 43.

160. Ibid., p. 17.

161. Colorado Voices: A New Chapter, Oct. 20, 2022. Rocky Mountain Public Television. https://www.rmpbs.org/blogs/news/iliff-school-of-theology-lenape-nation-book/ (accessed online February 2, 2024).

162. Id.

163. Decades after displaying book bound with human skin, Denver's Iliff School of Theology still working to make amends. Carol McKinley, The Denver Gazette, Oct. 2, 2022, Updated Oct. 8, 2022. https://denvergazette.com/premium/decades-after-displaying-book-bound-with-human-skin-denver-s-iliff-school-of-theology-still/article_29e32eae-4113-11ed-8482-9fbbaf77d202.html (accessed online February 2, 2024).

164. Lënapeí Pampil (Delaware Indian News) Building Right Relationships With American Indian Peoples Tink Tinker and Loring Abeyta, Denver Colorado, July 2022 PREFACE by Curtis Zunigha (enrolled member of Delaware Tribe, Bartlesville, OK), p. 5. https://delawaretribe.org/wp-content/uploads/din-2023-01.pdf (accessed online February 2, 2024).

165. Colorado Voices: A New Chapter, Oct. 20, 2022. Rocky Mountain Public Television. https://www.rmpbs.org/blogs/news/iliff-school-of-

theology-lenape-nation-book/ (accessed online February 2, 2024).
166. Lënapeí Pampil (Delaware Indian News) Building Right Relationships With American Indian Peoples Tink Tinker and Loring Abeyta, Denver Colorado, July 2022 PREFACE by Curtis Zunigha (enrolled member of Delaware Tribe, Bartlesville, OK), pp. 5-6. https://delawaretribe.org/wp-content/uploads/din-2023-01.pdf (accessed online February 2, 2024).
167. Colorado Voices: A New Chapter, Oct. 20, 2022. Rocky Mountain Public Television. https://www.rmpbs.org/blogs/news/iliff-school-of-theology-lenape-nation-book/ (accessed online February 2, 2024).
168. Id.
169. Id.
170. Id.
171. Id.
172. Lënapeí Pampil (Delaware Indian News) Building Right Relationships With American Indian Peoples Tink Tinker and Loring Abeyta, Denver Colorado, July 2022 PREFACE by Curtis Zunigha, Lenape Nation Chief + Elder (enrolled member of Delaware Tribe, Bartlesville, OK), p. 6.
173. https://www.facebook.com/GBHEMLEADHubs/ (accessed online February 2, 2024).

www.ingramcontent.com/pod-product-compliance
Lightning Source LLC
Chambersburg PA
CBHW011955150426
43199CB00020B/2870